COLLECTED POEMS
1938-1983

Books by Sheila Wingfield

POETRY

Poems (1938)
Beat Drum, Beat Heart (1946)
A Cloud Across the Sun (1949)
A Kite's Dinner (1954)
The Leaves Darken (1964)
Her Storms (1974)
Admissions (1977)

PROSE

Real People (1952)
Sun Too Fast (1974) (as Sheila Powerscourt)

COLLECTED
POEMS

1938-1983

Sheila Wingfield

WITH A PREFACE BY G. S. FRASER

Hill and Wang · *New York*

A DIVISION OF FARRAR, STRAUS AND GIROUX

ISBN 0–8090–3535–9 (cloth)

ISBN 0–8090–1500–5 (paper)

FIRST PRINTING, 1983

Library of Congress Cataloging in Publication Data
Wingfield, Sheila.
  Collected poems, 1938–1983.
  I. Title.
PR6031.O863A17 1983   823'.912   82-15531
ISBN 0–8090–3535–9
ISBN 0–8090–1500–5 (pbk.)

Acknowledgements

Many of these poems originally appeared in *The Dublin Magazine*, *The London Mercury*, *Time and Tide*, *The New Statesman and Nation* and *The New Statesman*, *The London Magazine*, *The Listener*, *The Times Literary Supplement*, and *The Scotsman*. My thanks are due for permission to reprint.

My gratitude goes to Mr. Douglas Matthews, Head Librarian of the London Library, for his patient and tireless work over many years. As it does, profoundly, to the kindness of 'Mrs. Paddy,' whose husband, G. S. Fraser, wrote the Preface. He died recently and I am more than glad that his widow has been so kind as to let me reprint it, the latest pieces having been read by him in manuscript.

S.P.

Contents

Preface by G. S. FRASER   xiii

POEMS (1938)

Winter   3
A Bird   3
Triptych   3
Young Argonauts   4
Highlander   4
Advice   5
The Journey   6
The Hours   8
The Heart That Leapt   10
The Dead   10
Chosroe the Second   12
A Lover's Contradiction   15
Odysseus Dying   15
Sonnet   16

BEAT DRUM, BEAT HEART (1946)

PART ONE   Men in War   19
PART TWO   Men at Peace   32

PART THREE   *Women in Love*   45
PART FOUR   *Women at Peace*   59

A CLOUD ACROSS THE SUN (1949)

Ireland   75
No Entry   75
Any Troubled Age   77
Architectural Tour   78
Analogue   78
Ross Abbey   79
Four Men's Desire   80
Sectio Divina   81
Origins   81
While Satyrs Hunted for a Nymph   84
Even So   84
Poisoned in Search of
    the Medicine of Immortality   86
Epiphany in a Country Church   86
War and Peace   87
On Looking Down a Street   87
Alter Ego   88
The Dog   88
Funerals   89

A KITE'S DINNER (1954)

Everyman in the Wilderness   93
A Tuscan Farmer   93
Lines for the Margin of an Old Gospel   94
Janus   96
Venice Preserved   97

Ease 99
Calendar 99
The Hunter 101
A Clerical Squire 102

The Leaves Darken (1964)

Darkness 105
On Being of One's Time 106
Three Saints 107
Cartography 107
Patriarchs 109
Continuity 110
Youth and Age 110
For My Dead Friends 112
A Query 114
On Reading What Happened after Noah 114
When Moore Field Was All Grazed 115
God's Nature, A Guessing Game 115
Hermes, Protector of Landmarks and Travellers 121
The Leaves Darken 121
The Foxy Smell of Fear 122
Village Seasons 123
With Palate for Fine Things but Penny Mouth 124
Miniature Paean 126
Cameo 127
Adam 128
Sonnet 128
An Answer from Delphi 128
Warning 129
Common Wish 130

HER STORMS (1974)

Glastonbury	133
Clonmacnois	133
Man and Beast	134
Not Forgetting Aeneas Sylvius	134
Tyranny	134
Cheiron	135
Carpaccio	136
Brigid	136
St. Francis	137
Murex	138
Ocean Through a Mask	139
Fifty Years Past	139
The Fetch-Light	140
Hope	140
Pitchforks	141
A Question	142
Blinded Bird Singing	142
One's Due	143
Back	143
That Altar to Pity	144
View	145
On Seeing the Pleiades Rise	145
A Melancholy Love	146
In a Dublin Museum	146

ADMISSIONS (1977)

Waking	149
Admissions	149
Any Weekday in a Small Irish Town	150
Mycenae	150

Dark Romney Marsh   151
Remote Matters   152
The Heavenly Twins   152
Ilex   153
Vanessa Cardui, butterfly   154
Bird   154
Sparrow   155
Narwhal Tusk   155
Eumenides   156
Rapunzel   156
No Rusty Cry   157
In Praise of Fashion   157
Were There a Choice   158
Nearing the End   159
Baby Song   159
The Oath   160

COCKATRICE AND BASILISK (1983)

Cockatrice and Basilisk   163
We Were Bright Beings   163
Caterpillar   164
Rose and Creed   164
Keeping House Together   165
Hazards   166
Blaze and Blackness   167
A Frightened Creature   168
Ferryman   169
Loving   169
Destination   170
Homage   170
Easy Felled   171

Thou Shalt Not Carry a Fox's Tooth   172

Urgent   172

Uncut Hedges   173

Song of a Past Scullery-Maid   174

Boxwood   174

All but Gone from Bermuda   175

Child   175

Unending Search   176

No Instructions   176

Notes   179

Preface

SHEILA WINGFIELD published her first volume, *Poems*, at the age of thirty-two in 1938 but the volume included many poems published earlier in periodicals and, as she says herself, 'My determination to be a poet was formed in the nursery.' In 1946, she published a long poem, *Beat Drum, Beat Heart*, of which Sir Herbert Read wrote on its publication (he had seen a newly printed copy left by his hostess in his room and it excited him so much that he lay awake all night):

> *Beat Drum, Beat Heart*, which impressed me greatly when I first read it about two years ago, strikes me now as the most sustained meditation on war that has been written in our time. I find it difficult to think of a modern poem of equal length that so successfully maintains such a unity of style and such directness of vision.

Yet there are, I suppose, many readers today who have never heard of this poem or of Sheila Wingfield's work generally. She published other volumes, *A Cloud Across the Sun*, in 1949, and a selected volume of old and new poems, *A Kite's Dinner* in 1954. I remember reviewing this with great enthusiasm in *The New Statesman*. Four or five of the poems in it seemed to me worthy of permanent places in anthologies of English twentieth-century verse.

There was a gap of ten years between this volume and *The Leaves Darken*, 1964, and it is only recently that Sheila Wingfield has begun to write poems again. The new poems in this volume, which are shorter, sometimes slighter than her earlier work, seem to me also more delicate in texture and more subtly oblique in approach. (The long gap was partly due to an illness necessitating a series of operations; Sheila Wingfield is still an invalid, in recurrent daily pain but, in the movement of her mind and her spirited conversation, the most active invalid I have known, other than her scholarly friend John Hayward, who, among his multifarious commitments, was poetry advisor to the Cresset Press and introduced that fastidious and now, alas, defunct firm to Sheila Wingfield's work.) I quote a short poem from the recent work that seems to me to illustrate that delicacy and obliqueness. This poem, *Remote Matters*, reminds me a little of the economy, the unstated implications, of Landor's wonderful last volume.

Remote Matters

As long as I can kneel to tell
Pin-eyed from thrum-eyed primroses
Or find a small cranesbill
In rough grass,
Why should I mind
If Dunwich is under the sea
With nine churches drowned.

There is not a word wasted there and the references are absolutely precise. Herbert Read spoke of the 'simple strength' and 'precise form' of the shorter poems included in *Beat Drum, Beat Heart*, and it is interesting to compare what I have quoted with two short poems from Sheila Wingfield's first volume, with its plain title, description and claim, *Poems*:

Winter

The tree still bends over the lake,
And I try to recall our love,
Our love which had a thousand leaves.

A Bird

Unexplained
In the salt meadow
Lay the dead bird.
The wind
Was fluttering its wings.

These, if published around 1912, would have been recognised as masterly Imagist poems in the manner of Ezra Pound or H.D. But Sheila Wingfield had in 1938 never heard of Imagism. It was her fate, and in some ways a lucky fate, to be a natural poet and to live, apart from a very few friends like John Hayward and like Ottoline Morrell in her late Gower Street days, quite outside the literary world. She sometimes deeply regretted this, but I think it helps to give her poetry its very special tone. No voice could be more individual, no personality more tantalisingly evasive.

Sheila Wingfield is something rather unusual in women poets, an objectivist. She is more interested in all the wonderful, sad, and glorious detail of the world around her than in herself; I, as a poetic introvert, preoccupied in poetry with my own feelings and sensations, and too inobservant of nature and obtuse about people to make any vivid picture of the world outside me, envy her that. This is not to say she is a poet lacking in very strong emotions, but that the emotions get expressed indirectly through her grip on the outer world. In this respect, the poet contemporary to herself she resembles is not any other woman, but an Irishman by birth who spent much of his life in England (Sheila Wingfield is an Englishwoman by birth who spent much of her life in Ireland): Louis MacNeice.

Sheila Wingfield has, in fact, described her theory of poetry much better than I can do, as well as the range of her subject-matter:

> As for subject-matter—the English and Irish country-side and country ways in general are so deeply rooted in me that I fancy much of this blows through my work. History, archaeology, folklore and the superb economy of the classical Greeks are other influences. These tendencies came together in forming my poetic outlook. This can be stated simply. What is personally felt must be fused with what is being, and has been, felt by *others*. But always in terms of the factual. Nothing woolly or disembodied will do. The same goes for events (which are in fact emotions suffered through-out history and in many lands). Personal dislike for amorphous description is shown by the 2,000 line poem, *Beat Drum, Beat Heart*, which compares men at war with women in love, and is in fact a lengthy psycho-logical-philosophical piece without any words used by experts in those arts. It attempts to sweep over whole cultures and peoples and histories—but invariably in terms of known or perhaps only suspected feelings, expressed in a way that makes such feelings recognisa-ble by a great variety of human beings.

MacNeice, except that city ways fascinated him as much as country ways, might have said almost all these things: and his greatest poem *Autumn Journal* does sweep over 'cultures and peoples and histories' (how the Greeks are different and long ago) as well as meditating on the coming war and exploring ruined love affairs. But he has a gloss and sophis-tication, suiting him, which Sheila Wingfield would think it vulgar to aim at.

Coleridge wrote to the Duchess of Devonshire:

> O Lady, born to pride and pleasure,
> Where gat ye that heroic measure?

The Duchess's verses have not survived in the canon and Coleridge, no doubt, was swept off his feet like many a middle-class poet before and after by aristocratic condescension. But though born to wealth, and married to an Irish Viscount, Sheila Wingfield found no 'pride and pleasure' in her lot. Her outer social roles find no place in her poetry and her two volumes of memoirs, *Real People*, Cresset Press, 1952, and *Sun Too Fast* (as Sheila Powerscourt), Bles, 1974, show her personality, as her poems do, indirectly, through the sort of person or incident that arouses her curiosity. The gardens of Powerscourt and the great house (burned down accidentally under subsequent ownership) alone sometimes touch her Muse. But a Dublin beggar can fascinate her even more.

She never goes wrong, I think, when she writes about country life; animals; pain, courage, or ecstasy. In some moods I find this my favourite among her short poems, and it would in my worst moments be a poem on which I could bite like a bullet:

Poisoned in Search of
the Medicine of Immortality

When Hsüang Tsung, great emperor,
Giddy and ill, carried in a litter,
Saw the stars sway,

His conquests and his arguments
And powers, falling into fever with him,
Pulsed their lives away.

Bow to his shade. To be at rest
Is but a dog that sighs and settles: better
The unrelenting day.

Sheila Wingfield has told me that she has no philosophy, and none is to be found in her poems: if to have a philosophy means 'to be at rest', she is right. But there is another wisdom, the wisdom of passion, of the endless search for experience and some essence in experience—whether of death or eternity—in spite of all pain. 'Better', and Sheila Wingfield, even swaying on a sick woman's litter, has exposed herself to it, 'the unrelenting day'.

G. S. FRASER

POEMS

1938

Winter

The tree still bends over the lake,
And I try to recall our love,
Our love which had a thousand leaves.

A Bird

Unexplained
In the salt meadow
Lay the dead bird.
The wind
Was fluttering its wings.

Triptych

From mulberry air which feels
Folded in thickness,
Her dress where she passes
Catching in spiked grasses
And glaucous aloe,
Her child and she, breathless,
Towards Egypt go.

Bleached are all noises
And brittle the mornings;
Chip of builders who cling
To golden scaffolding,
And shouts, will not drown
These tinklings and brayings
In Hierusalemes town.

Such greyness of misery
None else knows.
Three men crouch, asleep;
Still as a stone they keep:
The world in its plight
Cannot halt a cockcrow's
Curl in paling night.

Young Argonauts

In a small bitterness of wind
The reeds divided, as we felt
Our keel slide over stones, and smelt

The lough all round us. Soon the trace
Of shore was further than the sight
Of wildbirds crying in their flight;

But now the waves are paler finned,
The water blacker, we are blown
To somewhere strange and yet foreknown:

This is the Euxine,* this the place—
Row on, row on, to catch the gold
In dripping fleece, as they of old.

Highlander

And when he took his grief
Into the gentle-breasted hills,
He felt clouds marching, and the wind
Unheeded and unheeding pass
Through smallest bilberries in leaf
And the tough mountain grass,
Until he could no longer bear

The pressing of his soul,
And prayed to be released from self, from name,
To mingle senseless with the air
Some little time. But as within his mind
The oar would not desert its thole,
To his dark courtyard back he came
Uncomforted of all his ills.

Advice

I ask: can you no longer find
   Doors to the township of her mind?
   And are her thoughts, that like a cloud
   Of starlings wheeled with yours, too proud
   And single in their flight? You nod. So
   Cease your wooing; you should know
   Warm Daphne cannot be remade
   Out of the dark laurel shade.

Leave her; to wild islands go
   Or green-domed cities caped in snow;
   To roughened lakes whose yellow froth
   Is bitter as a god's wrath;
   Where nymphs, afraid of being burned
   By love, have into rivers turned;
   Or where through mountain gorges spurred
   A prince behind that golden bird.*

Now ride great rolling backs of seas
   To meet bright-cottoned ebonies;*
   Wander, uneasy as the tides,
   Until your renegade decides—
   Watching the chimney-cowls all bare
   And silent in the snowy air,
   Her forehead numbed by window-pane—
   She needs to feel your heart again.

The Journey

1

The ditcher as he cuts and digs
  And lays stiff February twigs,
  Thinks of his grate at home. But I,
  As cold as he is, must decry
  A countryside whose lack and stint
  Empty the mind. At night, a road-flint
  Seldom makes a boot-tip spark,
  And rolling mists erase each mark;
  While pollards in a flooded field
  Have their whole neediness revealed.
  As foxes are impelled yet loath
  To leave the dripping undergrowth
  That frets their nerves all day, so spring
  Drives me to restive wandering.

2

I will set out to journey through
  New lands or some deep forest; you,
  Will know how moonlit straits reflect
  Swans and not clouds, in an effect
  That cuts your breath. By several
  Opposing roads at last we shall—
  In park or theatre or the street—
  Be startled, yet prepared, to meet.
  Then will our joy be to divide
  The spoils we see on every side
  And as we travel on, to swear
  By the whole might of sunset, where
  Each tightly wooded hill rolls down
  Into the shadow of a frown,
  And trust in it where it can glaze
  A river with a gilded haze;
  To come to a great lake, and vow
  In silence, where the moon is now
  A loose-scaled serpent that must dance
  On formless water's blackest glance.

Leaving those towns of jostled cries
Where men have languor and quick eyes,
We wake to bells and to the chirp
Of unknown birds, and then usurp
A noonday glaring of white stone
That blinded Caesars, by our own
Dazzle of laughter. We'll acclaim
Ferocities of rock now tame
And husbanded, where soil and terrace,
Brown as an old gardener's face,
Wrinkle at dusk; and hear the slight
Tumble of fruit that measures night.
Onward again, more slowly, each
Warmed by some vineyard slope, to reach
Those empty mirrors, footless floors,
Where water fondles marble doors,
And in the darkness of an arch
Strange figures stand, while throngs march
On bridges with a silent tread.
But here our pattern must unthread
Its ended line, for suddenly
You leave me searching hopelessly.
An awning moves without a sound
In heaviness of air around
My head, as leaning from my window,
Chin in hands, I let a slow,
An undefended sadness fill
The evening and the night, until
A dawn wind, shivering the trees
By the unwoken houses, sees
My heart to be a swollen tide
Whose flood I can no longer ride.

3

Back from a whirling of white dust,
Back to where beeches shed their rust
Beneath those loaded, rain-dark clouds,
I note—away from talk or crowds—

7

A haystack's clearly shadowed cut,
The turned earth, and a friendly rut;
I grasp a stick of well-known notch
And smoothness in my palm; I watch,
Where winter oaks have always stood,
A pheasant slide into a wood;
I mark the hushed and bleak appeal
Of the long pastureland, and feel
The snow-sky like a pigeon's breast
Hold me entranced and repossessed.

The Hours

I

The hill lifts off her mist, as slow
As goddesses unrobe their feet,
And over spires and rooftops cling
The flushed veils of the morning's heat;
But gradually, to and fro,
We hear a pulsing in the street,
Rattle of window and of wheel,
Or cries, or river freshening.
Brisk and seaward in their flow,
The urgent ripples make us feel
A need to hammer through the world,
Or sail to where small islands lift,
To ride beside the wind, or shift
Great rocks that once the giants hurled.

2

Noon with his compass legs* will walk
Across meridians of the sea,
And for a while, watch with the hawk
A salty shrub in Tartary,
The council of the mountain crests,
A tortoise quivering a stalk
Of barley, or a man who rests

Under a Syrian almond tree;
And when the sun's unbarriered track
Reaches the downs, and from his groove
He slants his heat upon my back,
I pry through trellis of the vetch
Or spotted cloverleaf, and move
A forest with a fingerstretch.

3

Look from your windows, lovers, lean
On bridges in the warm, tired air,
For now is evening poised between
Light-hearted day and the dark's snare,
Like a girl flirting in her glass
And softly letting down her hair.
The little moths in seeding grass
Flutter their life out through the field
Where starwort gleams, and as you pass,
All colours that have loudly made
A dying declaration, yield
In whispers to the very shade
Of lichen, and of sheep that browse
Dimly below orchard boughs.

4

Alone among night-scented leaves
Must Sargon's daughter, pining, tend
Her charge, the Babylonian moon;
While others, like the leaning sheaves
That now in darkness seem to blend,
Make love; it is the hour when soon
St. Jerome,* putting down his quill,
Unlatches to the secret friend,
Then works, with all Judaea still;
When some will wake at horror's edge,
And women start the pains of birth;
When careful paws creep out to kill
And a bird twitches in the hedge,
While dreams smoke from the quiet Earth.

9

The Heart That Leapt

The heart that leapt
When, clapping suddenly,
Pigeon-wings escaped a wood;
Or while a boat heeled, trembling, to the sea;
That at the tale of the dog Argos wept
And loved the summer thickness of a tree:
Shame that it should
Be stilled from beating in eternity.

The Dead

I

The wind that blew the plumes astray
And bore the trumpet noise away
Has so effaced the dead
And thinned them to so fine a mist
That, harried in a drove,
They run ahead.
This wind, from barrack square
Or from the asphalt near some tenement,
Does it persist
In hinting that each mortal should prepare
To shiver in a leafless grove?—
A jealous wind, that will steal half
Of the hot meadow's reaper-clack
Which is all summer, or the night-stock's scent,
Or, on the road, a friend's laugh,
And pleases to hurl back
Smoke or broken tiles where urchins shout;
Which turns a sleeper's thoughts to untrue shapes:
A stubborn wind, that thickens till you feel
A door bang. And then memory's shut out.

2

The quiet dead,
Who were decoyed by a false tale

Of murmurings on Lethe's pebbly bed,
Have cast from them as childishness our joy
In live and woken things which yet, may now
Be part of their own foolish, constant dreams;
And are aloof from how
We long to peer behind the murk
And pantomime of bony jowl
And yew and headstone, to unveil
Their voices or their children's screams,
Or how they hummed and paused at work.
But tautly as you dare to strain
In listening, you only hear again
Hector to Aias calling like an owl,
At night, across the windy plain of Troy.

3

In spite of it, so many of us strive
With vigour, when alive,
For marks of perpetuity;
In spite of knuckle-bones that lie
In hills, grass shuttered from the light;
In spite of that Imperial road
Where warriors stand in their huge stone
And wildflowers blow about their feet; in spite
Of nothing being colder than the rain
On knees of monuments, or mute as fame
From trumpets with the angel gilt;
Though manifold can be a name
As is the wind's print on the seas
And yet will fade in libraries,
Or few as those in thymy air
Found carved on a Pentelic chair;
Though this one is as neat
As a lark's shadow, that one grown
To a forbidding, dark domain;
Yet do we want some tower built,
Be it of moving, marching dust
Where soldiers tried, and failed, to make their thrust.

Chosroe the Second

In bedstuffs of brocade he lies
Unmoving, while his shadowed eyes
Can only stare
Through darkness. For a screaming jay
Had flashed from his son's head
To take the throne as prey,
Keep him in his palace, and there
Starve him dead.

'The people smiled upon my son:
I feared and held his flutter in a cage.
They rose, imprisoned me; his rage
Making me carrion.
Oh, for the wind,
The bronze bit and the spume,
And earthy pebbles flying from our way;
Or could I lean
One moment from the windowsill
To snuff looseness of air that lies between
Orion and the medlar's bloom;
And cease to mind
That, carved in the bed's ornament,
These little squirrels still will play
Among their grapes when I am spent.'

So Chosroe grieves; until
For Caryatides he begs
With lifted arms and fluted legs,
To bear his sorrow through the night
On marble napes with all their might.
But from the pillared groves have flown
His twittering counsellors, and all

Is quiet as a forest, where alone
Slow-dropping fruits of hour or minute fall.

'It was a princely morning of bright winds
When flags, the horses of the air, were prancing mad,
That I inherited
The kingdom, glad
To send my armies striding like the sun,
Their cheeks now warmed by summer's grass
Of unknown kinds,
Now chilled by mountain pass,
Till Antioch and Damascus were outrun;
And leaving quays behind them bleached
Like bones, and streets dry as a riverbed, had reached
Chalcedon and beyond,
Three times. Then on to lands
For bases, among wind and sands
And creaking Phoenix palms, where the cicadas sing
Noisy as surf. My guards
Have watched the Hellespont, whose boats
When sailing westward
Touch salt-bitten leaves and seaweed floats
Up-river on the swell;
My embassies have been
Where little horsemen, for a moment seen,
Are swirled in mountain mist;
While here, as on a list
Of tumbled cities, I can spell
Jerusalem, whose shuffling crowds
I massacred to stain her floors
And take her Cross of the acacia tree;
Palmyra, empty but for a garrison
Who whistle in the open doors;
And unremembered spurs that winged me on
To the far hills or clouds.

' "Sire, I find the skies in doubt
And statues weeping."
Suddenly our lances in the field
Rattled like leaves October winds have dried;
Now hawks and partridges that wheeled
Above the dancing blades could see
Our columns—usually a stream
That in its flow one moment parts
For hostile, elbowing rocks—
Were trickles, creeping,
Nearly drained, without a gleam;
Now, loudly as the shingle knocks
Beneath a drawn-up wave, our clashing pride
Was overwhelmed; and when, at Nineveh,
My troops that had set out
All scaled in armour like a morning sea,
By dusk lay on the plain with smoking hearts,
I knew my kingdom fallen like a tree.

'Back into the earth's caul
I shall soon go,
Leaving this useless air
To some old villager
Who sits against his cottage wall
And plantlike feels the wind and sun.
You gods of light and darkness, blow,
Blow on my little spark, so nearly done.'

Then Chosroe puts his cooling lips
Upon the black flute of the night, to dream
That his own breath
Becomes a tune that, coiling, drifts,
Unable to recall its theme,
Until in gentle rifts
Each moment thinner blown, it slips
Into the endless spaces of his death.

A Lover's Contradiction

'I've known a summer morning when the rivermist
Would hang like Beauty's breath upon her glass;
Yet among streets where crowds pass
In living I persist,
And cry "Alas."

'Remembering far gentler waters, I regret
Their hush on a soft, sleeping shore at night;
Yet choose for pleasure a chill fight
With tides, and a stiff net,
And rain's bite.

'When gods were calling from the trees like birds, we were
At ease in our beliefs. But now the mind
Has come to open land whose wind
Lays bare; yet I prefer
It thus unkind.

'I want above all mortal things to hold my dove
And feel the murmur in her throat. You
Are but dark flight, the flash and sinew
And the fierce eye of love;
Yet I pursue.'

Odysseus Dying

I think Odysseus, as he dies, forgets
Which was Calypso, which Penelope,
Only remembering the wind that sets
Off Mimas,* and how endlessly
His eyes were stung with brine;
Argos a puppy, leaping happily;
And his old Father digging round a vine.

Sonnet

Jordan that feeds from far Mount Hermon's snow,
Thames with its fogs and warehouses and docks,
Dargle* whose alders dip on little rocks,
The Nile where heavily feluccas go,
Untroubled Avon in flat watermeadow
Or the mad pacing Rhine of many shocks,
Medway that swings the tackle through the blocks,
Deben now still, but for two boys who row;
The waters that will storm a city's gate
Or lie in glazing pools above a slope,
Or lessen, or become immoderate:
All these I feel within me and their scope
Carried by veins throughout my whole estate,
So quiet is my face and wild my hope.

BEAT DRUM,
BEAT HEART*

1946

PART ONE

Men in War

Shouts rang up the street
War War it has come
Like leaves they were blown:
A spear from its corner
A summons on paper
Or buckle to thumb:

In the dark of a room
Old fears were known
By wrinkled up cheeks
And by young wives
Bent back at the waist
To kiss them alone:

But light were their feet
As thoughts were broken
And barriers thrown—
Out of copse out of brake
Out of field they were flown
To the tap of the drum.

Goodbye the milkcart pony
Standing in the sun;
The creaking basket
Of a baker's round;
And summer's garden besom

Sweeping on the ground
Then pausing; work unfinished
And work done.

Goodbye to the inn's warmth
Of views on sport and crop,
Where each man's talk
Is well known as his gait;
Goodbye to what the village
Knows and hears; to that late
Word at the lit door
Of a small shop.

Goodbye to emptiness
That loiters up and down
To show its friends
The new pup on a string,
Or with some tight-held flowers
Goes mutely visiting,
On Sundays, in the cleanness
Of a town.

All this is gone, a lost age,
Gust-torn like a picture page
That flutters, sidles down, then lies:
For a new sight now stings men's eyes
As, carried in a wind that sweeps
Them over shores and crags—what steeps
They'll view, how take a city's height,
Where their force will next alight
Or like a spark will strike the sea,
Into what gates they bring a key—
Not one among the many knows.
But blowing hope, a trumpet echoes
Under arch of colonnade;
And shivering but unafraid

Other families will roll
With bedding and with bamboo pole,
Plank cart and piebald pony,
Jerking over hills and *li*.*
Look at them, at march or rest:
A gipsy walking gave the breast
To this one, and he likes to feel
Peril snapping at his heel;
While he, that Dublin bucko there,
At Liffey's edge who'd spit and swear,
Now whistles 'Killaloe' quite plain
Through the drenching Flemish rain;
Another, that in passing smiles
With pleasure at the red-curled tiles
Of homes; or he whose limbs are free,
Or knobbed like Kentish cobnut tree;
Pale Yorkshireman with eager gullet
And lank wrist—each one is yet
That god the Mexicans have sung
Who was in Paradise made young.
You will have heard some call them mad.
But whether any of them had
A doubt, which for a moment stood
Shy as roebuck in a wood
Before it fled in startled haste,
Is forgotten and effaced;
Or whether, to the night air
Extending patiently and where
Lyra throbs and Lynx spies
And Draco's coils anatomize,
Men turned for help, with dry lips,
Pumping heart, wet fingertips
And gulping breath—historian
Or plaque will never say. All I can
Tell is, that as clouds which seem
Too soft may harden till they gleam
Like iron shields, then clash their scorn

Downward, by veined anger torn;
As fire through Leinster's bowels ranged;
Or as the French king's blood was changed
Who saw the Englishmen at Cressy;
As a pibroch's wail would free
Some heavy sword from off its strap
Forcing the plaids to a tight wrap;
As on a gentle morning, youths
To whom a lute, a rose,* were truths,
Fought from thick-rigged galleass
With savagery that saved the Mass;
As those by nature wise and mild,
Twelve provinces of forest and wild
Rivers, terrors, ravines crossed
And mountains, half their number lost,
On the Long March* which lasted three days
And a year: so war will braze
My metal. I declare, that with the oldest
Of our ills pressed on me, borne on me like
   A storm which no mere plan can shift
   Or strength dispel, with danger turned
From a low thunder rolling in the hills
To an immediate hurt, I am aware
   No time but now ever existed,
   This was I meant for, here I am man:
Which—before a fox saw villages
Die out when the Euphrates changed its bed,
   Or lazy air first woke to tower,
   Or hunters could hear northern winds,
While grasses whipped their legs, or moaned in rocks—
Men learned, men knew, men felt, men understood.
   The fact is proved and clear, that war
   Rescinds what mattered, rends each form.
My hand, no longer casual and loose-plucking
Under a filtering of trellised leaves,
   With careful and slight trigger act
   Gives vast effect; wishes once scattered,

Vague as any drift of gipsies, have now
Gathered from their road and ditch and plain
Into one march of power; thoughts that were
Finches starting from a thicket
Wing to where the eagle and the sun
Beat fiercely in a far and dazzled reach,
High from the ground's indignity.
Witness how David, rid of foes,
Grieves most; and Caesar sets up Pompey's statue;
Over Alps how emperors can boast
In fight and Holy, then, be crowned.
O praise events that led me to this
Fate, whose searchlight-cone, or glint on hilt
Points out the place where I can show my whole
And candid self: let me be great,
Bold, gilt by that esteem
Each lover longs for in a woman's eyes
To flood his soul with bliss and to uphold
Supreme compulsion and desire
With governance, salvation, succour,
Monstrous commands, and favour. Let me die:
Cut out my heart and hold it to the sun
In fury; may its blood run slowly
Under root and stone of time,
To rise in temples where ash-whitened Shiva,
The abhorred, renews by fire; and urge
Crusaders in far massacre
To tread the winepress of the Lord.

Brothers, this is our cloud, our hidden night.
We, being obscured ourselves, know nothing,
In this darkness find no frame,
No ladder to climb in clear air,
No tap or chip of bricks on a bright day;
But lean together as if chained to pillars,
Under scourge from the whole world.
And now not I, but at all cost

The other, must be saved from harm. Look how
In chaos they are carrying a boy
   On strong arms, with safe steps, or lifting
   In the half-drowned enemy,
Their names lost like a voice in the storm, shown
On the scroll of the sea, hushed in passages
   And space of air, of empty windy
   Air, or shouted in a noise
Uncurling to implacable explosion
And then vanished, gone. Note, in this turmoil,
   How it's strange as myth to meet
   A man who sows his land in calm,
A pigeon nest, joy of a watermill:
For in our blood we feel the heavy pace
   Of cataracts and, in our limbs,
   The tremor of small leaves that shake
Beside them, on their banks, perpetually.
We are a madness, shrill over the ground,
   We are the bass notes' melancholy;
   We are the men who pulled Lorca
Between shrubs, beyond night-shadowed houses;
We are a man dragged and killed on the outskirts
   Of a town in Spain. We also know
   Much of the horror and the numbness—
Snow to the waist—of the defense of Moscow;
A shelterwarden's knack of seeming mild,
   His inner rage. Another time,
   Close under the soil we go
In trenches, huddled in a reek of furs,
Like pictures in a bestiary: for cunning,
   Fellowship and cruelty
   Live in my palms and shins and back;
And glitter-eyed, like flocks at night, are those
Who camp in dips and hollows of a field.
   Each thing that stirs, warily
   Is watched and feared and felt and spied,
And silence, or the din of gunfire, guessed

For signs. Sappers have kneeled; they tap and wait
And listen for the faintest sounds,
    Then know their fate. O smile O cry
For minutes hang on rumours of a rumour,
Hours fall to a wreck, and seconds beat
    As in Cassandra's pulsing neck
    With my defeat or with your doom,
With answer to our two encountered ranks,
With hurts, much longing, sickness and huge dread.

But look, how this one's glad and how he grips
His steel; nothing astounds and all is safe,
    Lightfooted, as once in a lad*
    Angel led and dog at heel.
With talent for his pith, fame in his eye,
He makes design and chance, by strength of touch,
    Agree like music on the map
    Of high campaign towards his end.
Then will the Incas blaze near to, like suns.
Rochelle unbend itself. Madrid give in.
    A prodigy. But in the haste,
    And in the clamour and the sweat,
This sharp acclaim is his own shout, the ray's
Behind his blink of tears: he does not know
    That over waste the dawn spilled out,
    The street abandoned when he came.
But I—what I have done has come untied
In spite of all I've tried or said. For long
    I fail. I can do nothing right,
    But heap mistake upon mistakes;
While war's old cart goes slowly creaking on
Into the disillusionary years
    Of its real destiny, where later
    My own enemy will tread.
Where is my cause, that seems as cold as a blown
Mist? It was so firm, so solid. Must I think
    It's I have grown into a ghost?

All is reversed; all is astray;
And reason an old mirror full of flaws.
Gestures that were heroic are remote
  As black clouds in a battle-piece;
  But they need rain in Barcelona
Where there's blood up to the second storeys.
God of hopes, how you misguide us. We,
  Who thought we had the heart and sinews
  Of strong beasts, of noble birds—
Head high the running stag, the great in pinion—
Find we emboss, with virtues and with oath,
  Only a blazon, cut in stone,
  And which the weathers chip and winds
Chafe. I'd said our coats would boast our pride—
But see, mine's foul and ragged with deceit
  Because, by Ronda bridge across
  The double cliffs that sheer to drop eight
Hundred feet, and from whose rocks so many
Pigeons flew, instead, the violated
  Nuns fall, fluttering.
We thought, this is warm, this is different,
This abscinds us from all past fights, as we marched among
      haycocks
With some of the brambles ripe,* but the same chill
  Lies on our hair, as in pale winter
  When the saplings are cut through.
Indeed, there's more of torture; and the crime
Of children with their peace hurled into air:
  More fault, more insult and more shame
  Than can be cleaned out from our core—
Unless Time, in its passage round the world,
Should, like an idle workman, make a halt.

When Jacob laid his head upon a stone,
Jacob of Aldgate, he was now alone

In the dear land of Judah. Here the guns
All day had uttered threats like benisons
Over a ground where love and sorrow erred,
As had the prophets that his father heard.
Here there was woe, here desolation came
Advancing long ago, showing her name
Nettles and saltpits and the voice of birds
In empty window-frames: and still could words
Of mercy, loving-kindness, goodness that must
Come, quiver in whiteness like hill dust,
To fade at night time, while through bushes ranged
The small sheep, restless, with their herds, unchanged.
All else is silent. As he turns on rocks
And olive roots, his memory unlocks
Some Reader chanting in a quiet stressed
By pages turned together as a forest
Quickly stirs its leaves; the careful tread
Of carrying the crimson velveted,
The red-wrapped Torah, through a muttered dark
Of men more shy and inward than the Ark;
Or, near the Minories,* the hint and fact
Of what man's wits can seize, know, make, transact;
A sale bill of old stock-in-trade across
A dirty shop front; and the grey hurry; gloss
Of rain on pavements; and each market friend
Who stood and argued, argued without end.
These are the last good things he will have known.
For should he live or die, all's twisted and grown
Monstrous from this force of arms; a force
Allowing as much refuge and recourse
As there was bastion or parapet
Against the treachery on Olivet;
A force more harmful than sore ages spent
Burdened by common ache of punishment;
Bringing no gain, nothing redeemable: instead
Blackness and rubble lying over Samson dead.

'I was a Greek. I climbed Aornos' rock for Alexander.
My foot slipped on the pine needles and my breath hurt.
Round me men hurtled down to where the Indus
Washes that great crag.'

                O men O commanders

'I lived by the Border. Mist would bead our woollen cloaks,
Our pelts and faces, on the mornings when we woke
Ready for foraying. I died in the grass
As lonely as a crow.'

                O men O commanders

'From Hejaz I. Much I endured of thirst and of sore eyes.
I rode for one who led us* and for gain, and knew
The camel-thorn, the clefts, the stinging wind
Of promises unkept.'

                O men O commanders

'I was a Catalan. I fought in hills near Teruel.
I was so cold and hungry. Who was foe or brother
No one learnt. Black mounds under the snow
Were bodies or else earth.'

                O men O commanders

'I a Venetian* whom the Genoese strewed on deep water.
Spars and oars of all our fleet had snapped like reeds.
I drowned, thinking of young fishermen
Who wade in a lagoon.'

                O men O commanders

    'Here is his picture; you can't see the smile.'
    The line of the nose is sad, and the mouth.
    'This silver frame is all his monument.'

He looks astonished. That one
Has lowered eyes, as if he knew.

'Sir, the patient has no face, and hears
Nothing.' But the small fitful noise
Of a hill wind is in his ears.

'They must have drifted many
Weeks before they lost hope;
Their bodies had no disfiguring marks
Of oil or sores, but were frayed and bleached
Like an old rope.'

Seeing great
Warriors in my head,
And how each yields
His breath in state:
Aruns with mouth against Etruscan asphodel;
The small waves, steeled and glittering,
Of Pompey caught in the shallows;
That stab to Brian, the old king;*
Beloved Sir John Chandos* on the field
In Vienne, whom the avenging,
Fighting knights can hallow—
I let out my sap,
With sobs, near rotted
Mangold roots that smell
As sour as failure.

Stumbling in retreat,
    The others, still with armed pack,
    Feel flints cut into feet,
    Rage at cobbles, curse their knees,
    Thinking they'd been fools to fight.
All's wrecked on either hand.

We can never talk
To others: who would understand?
The sight
Of plough up-ended, spoiled rick,
Scarecrow in a torn field,
Is fellow to this fanatic
Whose staring eyes and rigid walk
Keep by me like some dented shield.
How strange, these gables over us and roofs
In blackness where
The rain pours from the guttering,
This splashed filthiness of hoofs.
Cards lie scattered in a tomb.
Someone picks them up and sees
Instead of Queen and Jack,
Hector, Judith and *Lahire,**
Lancelot, Alexandre,
Who should have never left the womb.
French. Throw 'em back.
We hid, we ran, we had
To reach the water; then
Our oars dipped in to make
Eyeless sockets of a crone.
For heaven's sake,
How soon will I be let alone?
Past the thin trees of France,
Or in a wicked wind from side-streets,
Trail a rifle, drag your lance.
Dawn comes up grey and meets
A woman smiling at us, mad;
She puts a finger to her lips,
Shakes her head and slips
Down an alley.
Night will find the bare plain
We captured; there we crawl and press
Through dead ruins of our pain.
'My mind's root is bruised: all

I need is nullness
And to lie where I fall.
Everything will be so changed,
   I'll feel a clown, the cog
   Will never fit, I'll be estranged,'
   Fears this stalwart who upheld
   Enormous courage
   In monotony more wasteful
   And more weighty than steel wreckage,
   And as vacant as the air
   Round jealous soldiers' arguments.
A voice has yelled:
   Oh God, I dreamt I was where
   Women washed our bloodied garments
   Out, and looked at us through leafy,
   Latticed windows, and were sorry
   For us, endlessly sorry.
The last one,
   Trudging by his side, is thinking
   Of his grizzled dog
   At home, with ears back, blinking,
   Old and happy in the sun.

By any men who ever hung on trees
Or who were left, strung over wire,
To turn their heads now this way and now that,
Mire to their knees or groin; and by
The sour weeds on a father's grave;
By nettles grown near outworks of a fort;
By a church buttress which the hurt were laid
Against, their plaints heavy and broken
Like stone draperies of saints—
Never, never again.

By the square, tragic mouth
Of wrath, that may be shameful, hapless,

Or degraded by disaster; and by
Murder done in clean air
And truth wrung out, a dirty cloth;
By everyone who carried in his mind
Some bright image like a coin,
Yet could not give small change
Or find a right retort, surprised
And piteously;

By any houseless ones who sit,
Emptied of feeling, on a heap of bricks
And grit which was their all;
Chiefly by those who cannot sleep
But—fretting like the wind at night—
Think ceaselessly, had they advanced,
Gone back, been forthright, or declared themselves
Some other time, or place, or way, there would
Have been no utter, endless grief: I swear,
I pray, never again.

PART TWO

Men at Peace

Mist has fallen quietly on air
That once stirred past a mountain fighter's head,
And silent are the rushes where
A boy into Scamander* bled.
Hidden in the ground are bane
And warring; and the bitter groans
And orders and a leader's tread
Forgotten in the long rain,
Like little birds that hop among the stones
Of Hebrides and all lapsed islands.

'Under the alders
Just let me be;
All there is here
Is drip from alders
Into a lake
Of half sunk logs.'

How heavily white fogs
Will roll through fields of memory
To cover pain with northern balm.
Even this Southerner can seldom speak,
Now war is done but, sitting
In his courtyard, listens to the creak
Of chestnut boughs. Only a leaf will make
A shadow on his wall; the sun
And nothing else, can overtake
Thoughts which are too slowly spun
To snare the reason of each hour
Of living, or to understand
Why the clock shows in the tower,
Why the blood beats in his hand.

'From bed, I hear
Them sweep the morning's
Echoing street,
While the aged maid
Comes in to set
The washing ewer
On a chair.'

Somewhere in a field, there's short grass growing.
With an ear to it, one almost feels
The blades spring. The mind is prone
Or supine, and as calm
As this poor bit of ground
That carries signs of donkey-grazing

And the smells of summer, and that's bound
By walls so loose and easy-built
That much of them have fallen. Weals
Of many hundred seasons lie
On a great rock that's bare of bloom.
But all at once, senses and vision tilt
In shock at the stupendous sky,
Then down, to wonder—could this be the stone
That was once rolled back from a tomb?

      'O who can bear
      The brass and yells
      That shiver through
      The mended village, while they
      Shoulder flags; it grates
      Against the teeth:
      A blizzard in
      An east wind.'

Aeneas carried an oar inland,
Knowing the broken coast and pirate ships,
And where they asked him, What's that tool?
He thought it right for a new town to stand;
And as a bird inside a wicker cage,
Kept from all hawking doubt, uncertain rage
Of things, will stretch its feathers to their tips—
So vines may bud; and mirrors fill
With movement; after a trampling from a fool,
Spiders again may sling their webs in dew;
And rocky outcrops of a hill
Be taken up and cut, as men devise,
For arches to enclose some lengthening view;
While from the lazy meadows spires will rise.

      'Ted's father, leave
      The graveyard beside the canal;
      Put cap to head

As you wipe your eyes
With the back of your hand.
And you, leave the memorial
In the dark vault.
No love dies ever,
And no fault.'

Free from hateful foreigners—
The way they cut their hair or clear their throat
Or dig their elbows in one's private ribs—each
Is back into his old coat
And usage, land and life:
'Now we can own ourselves, like decent folk.'
In Wales, racked by rivers
That will silver its dark lore with rapid speech;
In the scant North, whose men and trees
Make strong and thrifty growth; in Suffolk, flat
As mud, where the slow-voiced have always spat
From barges beating into estuaries;
Everywhere, builders and their jobs in life
Can jogtrot on again like husband and wife.

'Contentment's when
An ache has cleared
And left us whole,
While from the borough benches
Ringing can be heard:
And Lateran
Or Lutheran,
The dear clang
Breaks into the soul.'

The sea has brought her dowry, and the tide
Has laid its jetsam all along the shore.
But up the hill there's cordial
And beer, new curtains, ashtrays that were coral
Found in a far gulf, and relatives

Crushed closely, joking, to admire the bride:
She will be shrewd and practical, and a just
Comfort to this fisherman who must
Tomorrow drag his trawler-nets once more
In rain, on the sea bed. The sunset gives
The guests, on leaving, music played
Along the crowded esplanade.
And later, a law-copier who lives
On deeds in unstopped verbiage,
Thinks of a past Regatta week,
Rest, and the ferry's shriek,
And sees the crawling wave upon the page.

       'How civil to dispute
       In neutral air
       Of judges' courts, dusty
       As a sawmill where
       The churning wheel outside
       Clanks in the same place to chide
       Whoever cannot make, assemble,
       Drive and gear together
       Lasting, hard repute.'

But here's a morning walked alone*
   By someone who, at worst, has known
   Work inside a tutor's book,
   And care, in dry or troutless brook.
   Past glinting bracken of midday
   Where only flies and midges play,
   Past a stone wall, past furzes mean,
   Past a straggle of boreen
   With dusty burrs and beechtree mast
   And fine fir-needles on it cast,
   Past tumbling plaint of notes that stop
   Him dead to listen, up at top,

Past tufted bog, and past the baulk
Of sloe hedge and wet bramble stalk
He goes, to feel the hours that lag
Beside him, run to the fore and drag
His wishes into being filled.
With wilds to alter, forms to build.
Soon drafts and invoices are stirred
By the numbed hands of agents in furred
Hats, or else by ledger clerks
Quick-tempered in the heat where barques
Ride and part the harbour scum
Outside; till vessels lately come
From Naples or the Baltic Sea
Lean against a Dublin quay
And from their holds pitch out large crates
Of statuary, railings, gates,
Amazon and warrior,
Head of pagan empress, or
Apollo with his sun's horns
That workmen think their Saviour's thorns.
Then for planks and platforms fit
To roll those pedestals of granite
Quarried in his own hills
In which the wind cries out and chills
The nesting plovers of Glencree;
For all must shape as perfectly
As this well-reasoned rockery
Of mosses over grotto's eye
Where, unseen, a trickle learns
Darkness through the dripping ferns.
Ending a path, how curious
These figures of fierce Eolus:
Like two great metal men, they blow
Their curving streams to merge and flow
Cross-rippled in a bowl; while out
Of a snub dolphin nose, or spout

Of lips, more veils of water jet
To fall in tiers, and then beset
Slippery shoulders and the charms
Of nymphs with shells and clutching arms.
Now all's finished, placed and still:
Nothing base and nothing shrill.
Here, stone shadows of a cup
To griffin heads are fluted up;
Here, acanthus leaves and horn
Of rams, on bronzen urns are borne;
Here, in sunk gardens, gods could sip
At this huge tazza's marble lip;
While there, the mounting grass succeeds
Terrace by terrace, till it leads
To pebbled slopes in black and white
That imitate each turn and flight
Where mules go steeply up and down
And laden, in an Umbrian town:
Through all, could no more come regret
Than wild hare with her leveret.
And so, by reed and lake, where the twin
Horses* prance in discipline
As, delicate of nose and leg,
They wing the air and seem to beg
Such loveliness to stay, by length
Of alley in the sun's strength,
By each invention and device
That tames the mountains at a price,
You'll wander, and by flickered shade
Of statues in a beech glade,
To let your inmost sadness fall
Blackly, under ilex pall.

So will a voice at random
In the fields become
A structure of compassionate sounds

Which you will climb like ladders in the air,
Until the mighty, fugal arguments declare
You noble, sad and great.

So, in a Gothic window,
Virtue with all force must press
In power. Unquenched, the embers glow
Round Peter's robe that's greener than sea deeps;
Saint Eustace aims his shaft as the stag leaps
Through the Cathedral darkness and the dread.

So, if a Londoner,
You go from Amen Corner*
Into Paul's, on up under the dome's
Vast hum of silence where the many tongues are tomes:
You sit among first books, and read, if you deserve,
Of *Troilus and Criseyde*, how the pen stabs with goodness
And undoes the nerve.

So someone will detect
And map proportions that connect
New threads of reasoning and light
Moving unceasingly in growth, or in the sea's
Suspense, in stars that comb the air with tracks
And problems as with parallax.

So the lens grinder*, blest in name, in soul,
In understanding of our load
Of human plight,
And for defining attribute and mode
Of God into one luminous, transparent whole,
Stays gentle and upright.

Such fruit, clamped to the wall,
Fills us till we're gorged,
Or till the rags tear

Or brads bend.
Have we by chance used
Nails the tinkers forged?

For look, philosophers have lungs
That choke on glass-grit, it's been proved;
And children scream; and old men steal,
Or die of cancerous tongues.
We dip slow oars of thought into the night
And find we have not moved;
And what are libraries? Can printed page,
Or even hassock and cold
Stone smelling of piety, assuage
My inner tide of doubt? Light
Is dimmed, the scene rolled,
Smallish dust blows from the stage;
And the dance of a young teague
With casual-cunning toe and heel
Becomes a ponderous Germanic gigue;
And where, by twisted fountain and by ways
So devious and delighting that the running gaze
Is lost, enchanted, in the sight—yet
The very stillness of the air's a fret,
A hint, a whisper of the growing
Need for some harsh harrowing.

A room where arguing intellectuals whine,
Then limply give their hand and start again;
Another, where the Adam-style pilasters
Echo with a self-important cough
Of old and knuckle-rubbing men who like
The softly lapping fire, the rustled *Times*,
After a hard day's hunting: those who once
Had felt at home in either, are aghast.

We'll go no more to the woods, they're now bricked up
And villas grow as campion by the way;
And all along wet tarmac hoardings show
In boredom, like the new and cleanly pub;
And a mock Tudor tea-house mocks itself,
Mocks hunger, and the fools who think that beams
And pewter jugs and cakes are carrying
Them daintily into a turbid past.

We'll walk instead on pavings and on paths
Where grass is trodden and the elms are doomed,
And dogs, the smart-trimmed and the mongrel dogs,
Play in the Parks, and small boys pitch their stumps,
And tramps unwrap things from a newspaper,
And women mince, and prams are wheeled along
For ever, under careless sweeping clouds
To the far roar of buses round about;

Or, from a City roof, we'll see how soot
Lies in the flowerpot left on a sill;
How iron rusts; and the eroded bricks
Rise up in grimy insult to the air,
Whichever way they're set; and humans live
As bindweed grows over a clinkered mound—
Here, and at back of equal towns whose streets
Such windows scan, while never a face looks out.

For now our thoughts are caught in thicket growth
Which slowly strangles them with age; they feel
Mute as the woollen horns, fixed as the chase
In darkened forests of some tapestry
Which has been stared at for no purpose for
Too long; being as stale and as exhausted
As the parlour walls, and yellow air,
And ticking clock, of all dead afternoons.

We have turned back from Tragedy, that land
Of warning and of storms and godlike speech
Upbraiding us, griping our mind and marrow,
As in the winter, trunks of trees seem twisted
One way by a giant's hand—gone back
To comic papers, and euonymus,
The promenade, and sandfleas on the beach,
And strum and tinkle of the Pierrot fools.

Once, in the dark of obsequies, our passion
Thickened till it grew to total might;
And once in childhood, over the wall to where
The river shone its promise in the meads;
But now, as salesmen moving through half lights,
We might be tired-out women traipsing
The rainy suburbs, on uneven heels,
In ugliness, unkindness and in waste.

Meanwhile, through institutions towering
Like their unending, shadowless grey days,
There's been amassed in record, ledger, file
And down long office corridors of fact,
Index and tabulation of our deeds,
So that all things are noted and exact,
Balanced, budgeted and accounted for—
Except that life seems pointless and disgraced.

By all ruined learning,
Where it may be:
By saint* that spoke
On small isle's space
Whose silverweed
Now meets the sea;
And Glendalough*
Where oar's stroke

Guides the tripper
Through deep rest
And quiet face
Of hermit's creed;
By systems of grace;
The good in all things
Confused as talk,
Or stray as goats
In cemetery
Of Muslim bones;
And Peter's pence
Crammed in a case;
Or Jews caught
In the Law's decay,
Who push their prayers
In cracks of stones
At the Temple's base;
By Christ so crippled
From what's been taught,
He calls for a crutch
And tries to walk;
And by each empty
Site in the heart
Once great, yes,
As Armageddon*
Was when manned
And walled apart,
But stared at, now,
Quite openly—
I know how much
Has fallen, how
Akhnaton's mildness
Slid like sand. . . .

Oh, lights are showing
In Guildford, and people
Are yawning for tea.

Whoever is in low
Relief, faintly embossed,
Take heed, take care,
For you will be erased.
No more is noon when the groom shaves,
Peace under trees, or safety
The gilt vanes of Penshurst
In the sun. But time
And place are strewn
With cloud, lost like fumes
Within a darkness fit
For burning rubbish,
And the knife's release:
It lops what's done
To let new growth swell out.
O that I'd bud and break
And truly live—for look,
What heroes make us proud:
Such as refuse, deny,
And with perverted strength
Draw back, or those
Who most abundantly
And warmly breathe, and use
Their love, and swear, and fight
Into the press of things?
Find me a cause
Or a catastrophe
To crack and shake the false,
The phrased, the laggard pleas
Of a restraining clause.
For now, thank God, no more
Dismayed by Death—
(I blushed to think of her,
Froze in the night, and held
My breath)—I'll fondly give
My seamless skin and know her,
Like a man.

PART THREE

Women in Love

Clearly as a fife and drum
  Down the village lane may come,
  As bells may suddenly be hurled,
  Or willow and the ash-tree sweeps
  Into greying gusts of fear,
  As it rains, as starts the wren
  Or suddenly a maiden weeps,
  So is caring ever near,
  Ever hidden.
              We
  Who watch a woodman split a tree
  To its pale heart, at any breath
  May feel love with one heavy blow
  Cleaving us from head to toe.
  Then life and the whole sky turn chill
  And set us shivering, as when
  Europa, with her friends at play
  In hot sweet sultry fields, away
  By the great creamy bull was led
  Along a bitter shore, until
  Her hair was lifted by the wind
  And over the dark ripples sped
  The two to rough-topped Crete.

Even the ageing, the wise-eyed,
  The disenchanted women; those
  Most unassailable whose prose
  Of peace is round them like a dress;
  Even the unforgetting ones
  Who'd let no further pain compress
  Their lives; and those whose memory
  Is faded like a token saved—

(That letter or that strand of hair
Which has lost all its power and sense;
As, on a wall, a sword can hang
Quite disregarded, yet engraved
With battle honours of the past,
And rust eats out what was immense)—
They'll feel its touch; and those who've tried
To act like vagabonds dispersed
In public gardens, through May's hush
Will find the dark red hawthorn flush
And warmth, will know the pang and fear
Of couples who year after year
Shelter beneath it, stand in thrall
Without a word, and wait for the first
Thunder drops to fall.

Exalt this giant cloud, this clash,
   This storm that shakes our inmost being,
   Cracks foundations, and discovers—
   In the instant of a flash—
   That what was old is fresh and strange;
   Exalt the boldness and delight
   Of finding that if in our lover's
   Eyes we stare, on shafts of light
   Like will, like sight, like air we range
   To every landscape of the feelings,
   Every climate of the temper:
   To an innocence of mornings
   Milky new, without a name;
   Or among dust and tracks that bring
   Us nearer to some ancient fame;
   Or to the icy wind and mountain;
   To hard deserts of a plain
   Where monks, in emptiness of heat,
   On rocks rasp their hems and feet;
   To the wild places; or to ease

Of rivers; or contemptuous seas:
In turbulence and risk.

For watch: wherever someone grieves,
    As on a terrace along which
    Scatter and skitter the dry leaves;
    Or on a foggy waterfront;
    In shops; or in the City square
    Whose starlings clatter by the thousand
    While at open windows, working
    Typists fill the answering air;
    In every time and place and land
    (Perhaps they've known the other stress
    Of stoical foolhardiness,
    But this time without heaume or casque,
    Sallet or helmet, as in war
    Their men—and they—had worn before)
    Do women, unremarked, alone,
    Stroking their forearm absently,
    Or most composed and easy, ask
    Only for the might, the nerve
    To love (for God's sake don't be grateful),
    To agree, give tribute, serve,
    Perish, or bear the brunt.

Where is the lumber-room of what was important?
The bric-a-brac of old feelings? Finished, put away.
And where the motes of ideas we breathed for our *now*?
Lost corridors, stray paths in the woods to our *here*?
Forgotten, of no account. In me, I feel
New space, new time, strangely askew and on whose
Axes spin my world, as you and I—
The man, the woman—tremble face to face.
The air is filled with power, hesitancy,
And awareness sharp as a blade's edge:

The lightest gesture, the least sign, can alter
Our whole fate. Opposed like this, we know,
We two, the other's soul is the most threatening
And immediate fact there's ever been—
You are so whole and real, he says, and keeps
Back tears; she, Nothing can stop the force
Of this great hour: I, as a woman, know
That from this confrontation a momentous
Grace or plight will come. It is the reason
I was born a peasant in the rain
Or one who trails her mantle through the hall;
Centuries have waited and prepared
For, with mimed passion and mock battles—
Yes, for this one and overpowering cause:
A cause whose glare lights up the skies and roofs,
Streets, spires and alleys of the mind
With an intensity so sacrificial
That its blazing flash and burning shadow
Fill with unseen, heroic acts. What
Can profane, he thinks, such faith as this? And she:
In finding you, I find myself, will cry.

For now I understand all twofold things;
How dark and light, matter and spirit, gut
And brain can be acquainted, how they accord:
Angel and beast in me are one: because
The midway heart is held between
What's private, base, and what's diffused and rare,
Binding the two as the sun's power can weld
The soil, where his foot rests, into quick life
With upper levels of the air. Through me
All contraries of grief and joy are strung:
I am rage and mercy, impulse and slow patience,
Folly and wisdom; I am the rain-filled wind,
The blade that suffers drought. I've tolled
A bell of duty harshly; groaned and wept
For mercy like a saint on a stone floor.

Some fear me, and of one I go in terror;
I am those Fates with scant hair and red eyes
And brittle bones, who so disdain the young;
I am the thread that stretches to be nicked.
I am a parody and extreme, but round me
Natural things are stupid, without substance:
People with idiot faces, in nameless houses,
Going on errands that can have no meaning.
Aloof from others, I still speak for them
And must fulfil them. Bending my ear to catch
The oracle, at the same time it's I,
Fume-crazy croaking sibyl, who predict it.

In full process, now, of secret planning,
Anguish and boredom—and again anguish, all the time
Feeling his presence and voice: at night when all's quiet,
During the racking day, but chiefly in crowds
Where I always think I have found him, or see someone like
        him—
Each faculty and each nerve (for he tests me in every
Thing at all moments), each vigour is taut, alert,
Made into a halter for triumph which now almost gentles
Up to my hand and then, will slip away;
Each fibre throughout my frame is used, with enough
Force and guile to wrench apart an empire,
Or exhaust the world with strategies.

Should anyone ask, Where are these battlefields?
Perhaps in the country house
Where a clammy mist falls over the garden,
Fills muddied lanes
And surges into an empty room.

Perhaps in some Park.
Municipal ducks, freezing lake,
Reeds like straw,
And an old bottle caught in the ice.

49

Perhaps by sand near prickled,
Sea-pitted coral rocks,
Where fond hope and insufficiency
Are the same as anywhere else;
While in the heat
Roads blind you with whiteness.

These are my Flanders, Valley Forge, Carthage.

Principles are my breath,
They fly like vapour from my mouth:
O I am mad, mad
As whorls of air round hills, chilled
By shining mountains before
Tumbling to warm themselves upon
The breast of plains; turning
In branches of the carob tree,
Then seeking shade and grace
Under a marble bridge, a causeway;
Mad as harlot water
Feeling, always moving, among
Palaces whose stone has
Stepped its weight into my arms.
My breathing is the raucous
Laughter and the clatter from
A Venetian supper-tent
Whose awning stripes billow to noise
And Negro-carried wine;
Untamed exuberance of limbs
Shaken by Voodoo Erzulie;*
Thickness of tropic
Fire from scarlet flowers
Whose leaves creep and thrust
And spike and choke each others' lives—
This air inspires me now.

I said inspired: fully
   I mean it. Each word,
Each event, shows me its own,
   Natural tact;
From chance, or proper command,
   I am the elect.
My devotion is felt as it watches
   The pale young preacher
Who climbed to the pulpit,
   A rose in his mouth—
And look how confidence
   Can lie in my hand
That's loose and open, power
   Along my arm
Smoother than lip of a shell;
   And how my gladness
Breaks the sea in spurts
   Of dolphin foam.
How easy to move, to act!
   Forebodings have fled
As bat-form shreds of cloud
   Escape at sunrise;
What was difficult
   Is plain as noonday
Heat in light that dazzles
   The lost marshes,
Over which our thoughts
   Shake in the air
Like larks: this light, strong
   As was the vision
That Aquinas saw*
   Who then fell silent
To dispute no more.
   This light gives glory,
Lustre, unity—
   Wakens the Future

From half-lidded sleep:
    Who, with his eyes
Near blinded by behests
    And glare, shuts them,
Deciding to impose
    The shadow of old
Debts, policies,
    And doubts again.

Within our curtained alcove
    We are so near
To stab each other: deeps
    Of uncertainty
Must hang between our heads.
    My destiny,
And yours, swing up and down
    In scales that give
No justice, only judgment;
    While we watch
Grave statements rise like dust
    Of war, havoc
From messages that stray,
    Fears from a freshly
Toppled plan; and then
    Observe disjunction,
Incoherence, lack
    Of sense: with pity
And the ancients' terror
    On our face.

'As through the field
Walked I and my true lover,
I did discover
Goodness in gateways heeled
By cattle, dreams in the meres
And hope in taste of clover.

Now all I need
Is to forget,
For since our quarrel
All in the world's a weed,
And tears are salt as sorrel.'

That slightest shiver of wind
    Before dawn is the shock
To my soul when it learns he has ceased,
    Yes, ceased, to care.
What blunder have I made,
    Where was I wrong,
To be shown that miracles
    Are past? What
Have I done, for retribution
    To come on me swiftly,
Savagely, and teach me
    That fortitude
Is no use and cannot prevent
    My being destroyed?
'*Pourrvou que cela dourre . . .*'*
    Had said a mother,
Bending to blow her nose
    In the Corsican gutter.

I bit into the day
    To find it rotten;
Would I could spit it out.
    Recriminations,
Bitterness, reproach,
    Have opened a gulf,
Have cracked Time in two—
    Time that in splendour
Of success elided
    Into long
Negations of itself;

Time that could be
Timeless, without front,
　　Without direction,
Pace or guidance; mixed
　　Until those Persian
Arrows* blackening
　　The sun, and children
Who fear dusk, are one;
　　A Time fed
By many equal founts,
　　So that the chirp
And clink and chattering
　　Of Spring were twin
To shrivelled sycamore
　　And the wet leaf
Of amber-dropping lime.
　　But now, sharpest
Calamity has cut
　　Its marks all round me.
Painfully precise,
　　Their steps and minutes
Cleave and allocate.

It's thought the Angel*
Said to the first woman:
　　'Now, walk slowly
From the garden, slowly,
　　For perhaps
You will be called back.'
　　But God has despised me,
I am no longer watched,
　　My thoughts guessed,
Giving anxiety, care,
　　Giving alarm:
But ignored. This is defeat

Unalterable,
This is the worst, the most
Unrelenting revenge.

The wet wind storms the branches
And trees shake; the same wind,
  Blowing where there are boats,
Jumps them against the mooring ropes.
  Unless the tree uproots,
Or the rope breaks, or I go mad,
  There is no leaving. When
I see him who has this contempt of me,
  I feel a hot wave of sickness
Then quickly, cold despair. I think
  How surely and easily
Could I have still held my advantage,
  Had I said this or done that;
And dreams recur, showing some new
  And splendid mastery
To give my pride a triumph in daylight,
  Instead of it cringing, begging,
Along tenebrous streets of the mind
  Where arch and girder are broken
And behind the dignity, degradation is seen,
  And stupidity, emptiness.
The friends of bereaved cities feel shame
  To look at them, they find nothing
Noble or great in devastation
  Of what was once entire.

She ran from the vast house* and her pheasant-shooting
    brother
Towards the light there was in learning, towards living.
Amused, eccentric, kind; a witty ghost, warm soul

And mighty to understand, slowly she'd speak or move
Or give her arm and look into the eyes of those
Entranced by her, to find (so her whole life, she hoped)
The superb effulgence, the total intimacy of two
Feeling minds. Most of them mocked her afterwards.
She was heroic. She died alone in herself as always.
The London pigeons wheeling in wind and traffic, the
      pressure
And pressmen at the church door, or inside: she was nowhere
      in this.

A second one's young, and as she's walking down the street
Whose windows all seem to have ferns in brass pots
Or elderly ladies at desks answering their letters,
Her swimming eyes are remembering collegiate leaves.
She can discern no raddled cheeks, no sagging body
Of some collapsed Fury, no terror through her calm,
As she passes these victims of double dealing, or of powerful
Respectability, these reprobates and bullies, examples
Of bores, or what is raffish, pompous or calculating.
She thinks the worst her dreams can ever do to her
Is fail to show a mask of leaves, a crumbled urn.

A third one* sees her tended, heavy-scented garden
From the verandah. A dog yawns. A cage swings.
No defect of paint, no spiderweb, no branch out of trim,
Not a blemish on a waxed table, not a dab of dirt in the
      kitchen—
And yet, under this bland and meticulous order, the blister,
The shaking thread, the imbalance, the blame, the horror are
      hidden
But always in mind. It's fifty years since there was a man
Who strolled and whistled, quick and carefree, like the whip-
      ping waves,
Whom she would have gone with, now as then, anywhere—
To a strange land with the wind rattling the window panes.
'Come on, dogs; well, little bird?' and her hand trembles.

I can see
Berenice dragging her robe
Between bare pillars
From the sun;
Heloise a nun
Still unconsolable;
Kind Dorothy* enduring
Mist and rocks
Colder than those of Cumberland;
And Mary's letters, sweet* as phlox;
While Harriet has a scent
Of water's edge
Where now the pert
And nervous mallard and teal
Are watched by Parkgoers
From a gravelled ledge
In air that's brisk and fluent.
But for my loss of heart,
My pain,
There's a tapping
Window blind, or
A muddle of rain.

Let me slip away or sleep
    Or die. How can I go back
    Into each day's
    Queasy remembering?

I envy the very old
    With their faces wiped clean
    Of moods and movement;
    No pulpy flesh under the skin:
    Only a covering for the skull.

Women who are silent in manner,
    Or wildly frivolous, or crazy,

Or dispirited, or merely aimless
And vague—do I seem one of them?

The ravaging
    Use of feeling and valour;
    All the uncommon goodness
    That's been spent,
    Laid waste.

Look at the tattered room
    Exposed to the sky.
    No splendour in this ruin,
    But shame in small wallpaper
    For all eyes.

The mind is open,
    Desolate, swinging in the wind
    Like a squealing gate;
    While autumn woods all smoulder
    Till put out by rain,
    And pigeons clip the empty air.

There's nothing
For an edifice. Not even
Such small figurines* of clay
As are found in a tomb on the hillside:
Children, shawled and capped,
Carrying sheaves and dancing.
No weight is left, no tenderness,
As on a sarcophagus lid
Where man and wife lie knee to knee,
His bracelet twining on her wrist,
His marble fingers
Curving round her arm.

By our crawling
Spaniel-race;
The lash of our remorse;
By brutish things: snouts
Grunting at Circe;
Gaze of wrong
From mottled venom-face;

By the stretched tendons
Of the two robbers;
By him who thanked
Or scolded each person
More deeply than soul
Ever since or before;
By the women who stood
Beside those nailed planks—
We who spoke low
Under our hoods—
For pity's sake, no more.

PART FOUR

Women at Peace

Round my whole mind, the same
And snowy landscape lies
That once came with its blank
On Tobit's worried eyes
And gently covered up
His troubles. Earth is sealed.
Dead still the staring-coated
Bullocks in the field.
Stiff is each reed, each twig
Unmoved, each trickle stopped,
Unuttering, and seized

With numbness where it dropped.
Level and like all things,
Which way I turn my head,
With only a hunched bird
To show there's roof or shed
In country as well known
To me as home. But should
The scene thaw out, and I
Then wander by a wood
Or undergrowth of coppice
Fenced with ash, by farms set
Tightly in the weald,
By empty branches' net—
Still will the leaden road,
The sky, the death of sound,
The slaty cold and dumbness
Keep my senses bound
As in a trance—until
One morning when I wake,
Wake suddenly, not knowing
How, not knowing why,
Feeling a change to climates
Nearer South . . .

   Clear, clear
Like a young cockerel's cry,
The singing of a boy
Along a hill.
   I listen,
Free as this easy air
So thin, so clean.

   In the dark grove
Of mandarini trees
Under my window,

Snicking clacking gardeners
Take up the snatch of tune:
They curl it, turn it
And repeat it till it's twisted
Like the under-branches
They are cutting.
After that,
A little raking.

No more
To be watched
By high and hungry gods,
But to feel light, drained;
To move about as I wish;
To get beyond this garden
To the wild slope.

Lying in its grass,
All I can hear now
Is someone smacking a carpet
Far off, beyond the water tanks,
And very faintly
Children's cries.

There's no more need
To run aslant the world.

Meanwhile, elsewhere: 'I don't care
A kick of a hen,' says this one.
'The cold clank of the bucket handle,
The rat running on the wall,
My mother who hasn't a step in her since
She broke her thigh, the turf-smoke
And my face concealed in it—
All these are good enough.'

Another: 'Let us stop heroic
Lies and allegory. Too many
Statues have baton and blank eyes
Directed over the market-place;
Even the emblems—eagle, winged lion—
Of Evangelists, fail
To convince me: I prefer
A plover in a field,
The cat curled in a grocer's shop.'

The waves of Galilee have mirrored
Rosy-imaged oleanders
For an age. Along the shore
Magdala,* a mud village with fowls,
Has forgotten Mary. Sabras
Now help deepen rough red furrows,
Making a heritage,
An orchard crop, for boys and girls
Pale-haired under this sun
Instead of dark as ghettoes.

Each day is dependable and
Controlled, like an office clock; steady
As some figure with black skirt
And black umbrella you see move
Among the cloches, quite orderly,
In rain of Paris suburbs.
Reason, in charge of itself, craves
To build new colonnades of thought,
Or prove a spangle-lit
Fresh spark of theory, or free
Old proverbs from the humped *tels*.

If one could see beyond house fronts
Into the past, as through a pane

Of glass, the tremendous roar, then quiet
Of dying in rubble would be plain.
But beams and bricks are up again.

Under Crimean harbour depths,
What silent traffics go between
Sunk Greek galleys, green swaying weed
On marbles of the Chersonese,
Out-of-date warships, rebel cruiser,
Engine parts of every kind
And bones odd sizes—all of these
Washed like cockles of the sea?

In streets where paper blows about,
A stab goes through me of the talk
That brought disastrous happenings,
The death of feeling that I caused.
Urchins playing give a shout
And the thought leaves me as I walk.

Gone is anything sick, sad or fanciful.
What moved me was the hand of the Mechanized Chessman,
Horror and mystery in his stuffy robes.
What I've been through was the Hall of Mirrors,
Distorting mirrors of a fair. What I've seen
Were obscene freaks in a sawdust pit,
And scenes painted with size, swollen
The size of hallucinations—
All believed in at the time,
All suffered as one suffers
The anaesthetic dream
Of spiritual blessedness,
Of spirals choiring:
Then afterwards,
The fit of weeping.

There's a small hill on the Bog of Allen
With jackdaws and beeches and a square house.
The maids are by the fire. They sew and speak
Of a cousin, or how to help the niece,
Or will Dolan sell, or of the boy
One of them went with (as she bites a thread),
Or else the time long back when they found
An empty can of tea and some sandwiches
Wrapped up in a *Freeman's Journal*, and left
By the ambush there must have been at the gates
(And the mistress in bed seeing on the wall
The flash of the fired barracks across the way);
And will her great-grandchildren, they wonder,
Take after their da?
                      It's to be hoped they will,
Thinks their mother (keeper of all things
Who has watched her children sleep) who now watches them
With their father making a garden bonfire.
He's grinning and swearing under his breath
And tearing his coat and telling them how to help.
Screaming, happy in doing something,
And bringing the wrong sticks, they'll now and again
Take fright at the blaze, run away to her, then
Forget and dash back to add more. She looks
At their napes, at the back of their knees, and sighs:
How to guard them from danger, from fear,
For ever? The dogs go off to sniff and to hunt
On their own. Smoke tingles and eddies
Through sparks of laughter, gusts of seriousness
That are insubstantial and flickering
To anyone else—but to her, solid
As each farm building in the yard.

Leaf upon earth, and loam under the frame,
And pear, espaliered, nailed across a wall;
The chatter of small-territoried birds,

Or a staked plant that where it blooms will fall;
The fly crawling up a stem it hugs;
Beetles that drag their carapace, alone,
Intent, through thickest grass where groundbees drone;
A swan that dents her breast against an edge
Of lake, her feet now softly on the ooze
And now her bill nudging in roots of sedge—
These are my kin (she well might cry), their labours
Are my days and reasoning: as strong
And logical as schoolmen after long
Disorder, wreckage and dark anarchy.

We will now do the linen. The weight of it, lifted out of
    deep drawers
  And cool to the touch, and the warm smell when it's taken
  Out of the airing cupboard, give me a pride
That any woman has felt who's putting a room to rights,
  Scrubbing as if herself were being scrubbed,
  Scouring as if her soul were being scoured,
Straightening up and sorting as if in her own mind.
  (My helper, bending her neck, shows tendrils of hair
  That surely her friend, who has his bicycle propped
This instant against the ivied wall, admires. Let him wait.)

                            How good
To spice and flavour well; to walk the dim and white
  And dairy-smelling passages; to look
On harbours, as in Boston, when the fishermen are home
  (Their boats are *Evie II* and *Maria Soccorsa*
  With dories slung on the pilot-house roof, the snow
Filling them)—to be safe, and have enough for the fire.
  Or beside other quays where in markets, we women,
  Scarf-faced and red-fingered, must sell fish:
This is also good, the mist mingling with our breath
  In gossip and curses, to rid us of old shames
  And old mistakes that make us groan at night.

Crones stop in the street and mumble
  In each others' faces;
  Their grandsons are masons perched
  And painting overhead;
  Their nieces are washerwomen
  By stones of some broad rivermouth
  Dried to a mid-trickle.
In a room with drawn blinds
  Loneliness is consoled
  Between covers of the Bible:
  Often you only have to grasp
  The book to feel worthy.
D'you notice how old women
  Who have missed a destroying
  Happiness look away?
  Whereas the old and plain who meet
  Your eyes, do so because
  They know they are more holy,
  Or else more powerful—
Even if they've acquired
  A look of snapped twigs, or hollow
  Beetle-sherds, or gnawed
  Husks, or have about them
  A faint, discernible smell
  Of mouldering earth and deadness.

But growing girls: slow airs
Of cowslip warmth blow from you.
  Some, whose pairs
Of breasts are tightly met
Together as young apples,
  Will perhaps get
Caught by gasp and relish
Of mock struggle, and
  Become a prudish
Housewife or a drudge or
Slattern. You, the rest—

Whatever your
Demeanour, epoch, dress
And voice, timid or dowried,
   Ones no less
Than waif or heroine—
Are sisterly to those
   Who moved in muslin
On a tender lawn;
Who left the art-room, its chill
   Casts undrawn;
Outgrew a corridor
Of pianos practising
   In muffled war;
And who forgot the yew
As hiding-place. Your state
   Is strange, new,
Unhurried as the run
Of angels, neither ended
   Nor begun;
Your thought the shape and shade
Of soft air through a marble
   Balustrade:
Untried and unexpressed,
You wish for marvels, danger,
   Deeds unguessed.

If I could be like Niobe,
Mother of many, before the vengeance,
My robes brimming out with goodness,
Filled with content . . . But I cannot.
Something weak and nagging in me
Causes me to turn my head,
After a time, at any noise
Coming from far off, carried
By the wind from places where,
If you're in trouble, the old whore

And the old soldier, blunt, blowsy,
Plain as plain, are to be utterly
Trusted; where philosophies
Are arguments it's best to forget
Or else to remake each hour, and feel
Alter with a change of light,
With new work started, or the sound
Of sudden wet, below, in the street.
Lately, I notice that the flattened
Saints no longer burn their windows
But are idle and remote;
And I can't bear to watch the winter
Smokiness on playing-fields;
Or poverty, like a goat in its range
Over the common, along the waste:
And though ill-humour and a certain
Haste now hover in the air,
The day dangles an empty bridle.

'Hidden in the womb I lie
With beating heart and closed eye,
Thinking forward, casting back,
Through our living almanac.
Covered in as warm a tide
As this, and lapped from side to side,
I was washed in altered forms
By huge calms and vaster storms
Of that primal, misty sea
Tasting of futurity.
Gone my gills—but see their cleft—
Made when mountains would be left
Higher than the lakes which fell
Into gloom of bitter spell.
I have been near scale and quill,
Furry chine is with me still;
Seen the rocks and plains dissolved,

Seasons, heavens, aims revolved;
I have reaped bread from a weed;
Searched to find out every need
Of my horror or my trust,
Ecstasies, constraint, disgust
And then rebellion. Fortified
By great portents, I have tried—
Using all my brain and force,
All my will, all my resource—
To shape my life within a scene
Already known. In truth, I've been
Vain as cities, poor as hills,
Travelled through such endless ills,
Through such hope and fear and rage
For an unremembered age,
That I beat my prisoned fist,
Angered that when I untwist
From this closeness into air
Final and fulfilling, there
I must barter, prate and mime
For a pulse, a blink of time.'

How we hate each other
In a narrow room,
   We terrible knitters
   Under the lamp;
How we knot and lace
The hours interminable,
   Intricate and
   Pale as in
The Book of Kells, we nuns
And all unmothers of men;
   Or we who look
   At backs of houses
As we sit and stitch,
Crowded elbow to side,

Handling the stuff
And stiff brocade
Of death: for that is how
It seems to us who stifle
   Here, bound
   By a weight of days;
How we regret not seeing
Leaves in an approaching
   Storm fly up;
   And how we envy
Those who like to rustle
In their silks, and thread
   Words with looks
   Brilliantly false, before
They praise, thank,
And yawn to bed.

Solomon kept chariot horses
Stabled under Temple walls.
They stamped within their hollow stalls.

I must escape, I must avoid
The puckered mouth and twitching thumb
Of Age who waits for me to come.

Swifts flicker round the sill,
Beat their shadows on the blind,
Beat their hurry in the mind.

         She has reached
         The rim of time
         The dune end
         Of the world.
         Spiked grass
         Loose sand

What to lean on
Where to turn . . .
Something recalled
Before it is known,
Old as the ground,
New as herself
But sharp and steep
As memories
Of crag and shelf
In witless sheep
Who make their mountain
Tracks on a low
Mound, of rushing
Wind in ducks
Who are now placid
On the pond
But once were wilder
Than the air—
Some voice in her
That tries to find
And utter the old
Chants, the old
Pain, cries out:

O random Fate, who rout
And shatter and unbind
The elbow-leaning, tame,
Demurest pieties—
Free me that I may wear
A yoke I hanker for
And name: precise belief
In the authority
And overbearing deeds
Of a loved mortal, one
Whose strength and tongue shall be
The provenance of right;

A part in all transactions
Of his mind and any
Tragedies which follow.
Admit that the devout
Must have sanction from Church,
A thief from others' failings,
The privileged from custom,
Scholar from book—and I
From discipline of great
And terrible truths. Hold me,
Pour back my soul, let me know
Life the unfinished: so
Reflood the desolate ebb:
Renew me, make me whole.

A CLOUD
ACROSS THE SUN

———————————————

1949

Ireland

This is the country
That has no desolation, no empty feel
(The pagan kings are always there)
In ruined abbey, ruined farmhouse,
Slab of cromlech, or a wheel
Travelling a bog road
Through Calary's too quiet air.

No Entry

1

When Hector's foot comes creaking on a stair,
Or Helen's breath steams in the frozen air,
   Moments that no one ever sang:
   These are the hidden places where
     I move about and find
     Some freshness for the mind,
   A gap to be explored with care,
As over David's harp in a dark corner
Runs a mouse and gives it a small twang.

2

Constricted space! Others, I know, have wide
Imaginary fields where they confide
   Their dreams and where they roam at ease—
   For little Hamnet hasn't died,
     But makes a swing with other
     Children; look, Leander
   Steps out backward from the tide—
Not only dreams but systems of escape
As furious or everyday as these:

3

She's thin and sallow. The headmistress pays
Her meanly to curb the English pupils' ways:
　　Tenez-vous convenablement.
　　Outside, a château park decays
　　　　With drifting leaves, in spite
　　　　Of drifting girls . . . Then flight
　　To her room—the *Nuit de Mai*—to gaze
At the full-bosomed Muse, the poet's brow
And welling sadness—*Ah, quel ravissement!*

4

Young Ted, the garden boy, unsmilingly
Will trench and stake and dig. I'll lay a ready
　　Bet he'd never swear or fight—
　　With summer hanging heavily,
　　　　Or autumn smelling sour,
　　　　When colder winds scour
　　The earth, or shoots break out. Instead he
Glows, he burns from direst sin's repentance
While he shouts and moans on Chapel night.

5

That tramp, dirty as all London soil,
Hugs a park bench, his hideous face a foil
　　To children, birds and dogs, whose scufflings
　　He's too motionless to spoil.
　　　　Let the weak winter sun
　　　　Show the tree's skeleton,
　　The sharp leaves' scurry and recoil,
And daze his red-rimmed eyes and part his lips
As peace swoops to him on her pigeon wings.

6

Or other ways of sidling, groping back
From the affront of living. Almanac,
　　Great pyramid and portent turn
　　The sluggard-rolling zodiac
　　　　Into 'What month, dear, were
　　　　You born?' and 'Now it's clear,

We add . . .' The invisible tide is slack
And lost Atlantis silent; but those ears
Catch auguries which drown them in concern.

7

Even the Libyan Arabs* take retreat
To their Green Mountain, up a thousand feet,
   Their grazing lands. But I'm shut out:
   No entry, even by deceit;
      Not with my eyes clamped tight
      Against the speckled night;
   And never in my work, whose beat
Hurts with its knock and actual daily pulse
Of stinging joy, short ease and constant doubt.

Any Troubled Age

O mussel-coloured houses by the dunes
With fluttered boats feeling among the shoals,

   How many times can it have happened,
   How many times

O mountain straked and softened by blue air
With trickles fingering between the reeds,

   How many times can it have happened,
   How many times

O cottage field warmed by the breath of sheep
When rain begins to gossip in the hedge,

   How many times will woman see
   Some man trudging

To the door, and rise, with a broken welcome—
For the whole news has travelled in his eyes.

Architectural Tour

A pillar wrecked
By sand; the slat
Of softest leaves
To hide a voice
And hint its echo;
Pediments
Where hogmaned ponies
Prance in fat
Of stubbornness;
Or the stones
Of Clonmacnois,*
Lichen-flecked;
Cupolas that
Burst through snow;
Spires where angels
Catch their gowns;
Tin-roofed chapels
In sick towns —
A choice,
A guess.

Analogue

I

Men who care for the slow
Headswinging walk of a bull;
Whose hopes and dread rise
In the blade, bend with a stalk,
Who will explain each whim
Of angered, joking Fate
By marrying season to proverb;
Their hands knotted and learned
In lifting a pick; who know
How pain and weather can baulk
All plans: such folk, when dear
Demeter's ground lay warm

And dry with almond husks
And myrtle and would owe
Remembrance to the dead,
Argued, as men today
Talk, in *The Barley Mow*,
Of ghosts and penalties.

2

Men whose faces are stern,
For the rungs shake under them
As they climb different ladders
To consolation, and turn
In dispute or vertigo:
'Credo', they call like birds,
Then, 'Curro'. Aware of doctrine
And the great hazard of words,
Their skin creeping, their nerves
Taut in effort to learn
For certain the logic of grace:
Beside a gas-fire, in cloister,
Study or abbey—shut off
By intellect from the day,
Not heeding if last night's rain
Harmed or was southerly kind
To the breeding earth—their concern
Is souls and punishment.

Ross Abbey*

The cowpat track and dusty bramble leads
To childhood's riverwet and glistening meads.
O dear Ross Abbey! ruined, with a tree
Grown through you, how your presence lived in me
With images, persistent and devout,
Of a loved brother, weed and frog and trout,
Until that middle-aged, that rainy day
I saw you once again, then looked away.

Four Men's Desire*

John the Baptist stood with hair
Blown through by the morning air.
Calloused, lean as thorns and brown,
Over the bare land and down
The listening ear of time he spoke
A prologue nothing can revoke.

John, the son of Zebedee,
From the sweet Tiberian sea
With its kingfishers and quail
And oleanders, rips the veil
Of laziness. Through streets the crowd
Argues with him strong and loud.

John, asleep at Ephesus,
Stir your jaws and pray for us!
Pilgrims to your holy ground,
We're dazed by love, already bound,
And waiting to be subtly kissed:
O preacher and Evangelist.

John of Patmos, round your isle
Waves clash and suns revile
As you mouth, with roughened lips,
A barbarous Apocalypse—
Great visions of a lunatic
Who finds a world convulsed and sick.

First, vague prophetic sounds
Till a fisherman astounds;
Then a contemplative love
Transcending what all deeds may prove.
If last, disintegration's fire
Should come, we've seen four men's desire.

Sectio Divina

The heart sings
Of Colchis in whose forests once wild aurochs hid
   Till Jason* ploughed with them—
   O happy farmer Jason;
   And the splashed hem
   Of barefoot women on
A shore, stooping, looking for octopus or squid
  While the sea rages to condemn
   All tamed and gentle things.

   Because of savagery preferred,
   Gone the lost cause, the trusting bird:
   Gone the cahòws* and their strange cry,
   Gone from Bermuda; in our eye
   Life's image lies reversed, while slaughter
   Rules the air, the ground and water.

   Cures are found
In plants, or else where beaches lie most derelict.
   Gaze, soul, at the spiral
   Of a shell; count
   In the fircone's numeral
   How gnomons* can surmount
Opposing forces with the mediating, strict
  And Golden Mean, whose wiles are all
   Displayed in tide and ground.

Origins

I

   Thinness of music far away—
   Repeated thuds, a few high notes,
   Are all one hears—how well this teases
   Memory, angers the brain.

Towards me in the same way floats
A sense of forbears long ago
Distressing as that distant playing:
For it can never be made clear,
What did our predecessors fear?
How did they sleep? When did they smile?
Were they uneasy in their souls?

2

A wind blows along the quays.
Rigging slats. Hawsers creak.
Here they stumble: in big hands
Smaller hands that pinch and tweak;
Coming from the barest mountain
Or a quiet of flat lands
To cities smoking in the dusk,
To pestilence and grime that's both
On water and the merchant-desk:
These ancestors, these falling leaves
That as they rot make green my growth.

3

Before them—pedlar, diplomat,
Landlord, peasant*—these talk low,
Whistle, curse, stamp their feet;
That one greasy as his hat,
This one laughing from conceit.
All mine. As for the women: some
Have a scent of melancholy sedge,
Or laurels in wet woods; others
Rock slowly on high balconies
Under a charring sun; and some
Are rags along a gutter's edge.

4

Could quick, varied contradiction
Of a mood or thought derive from difference
Of fancies they were racked with—could
It stem from their belief in arches

Made of angels' wings, from fret
Of learning, or from schemes sad
As rain falling from winter larches?
And some ghastly call of wit
Come from where there was a joke
Before a murder—now where flit
Jackdaws in the ivied tower?

5[*]

Beyond such silting up, such tracts
Of time and back to paradisal
Leaves: this moist and sheltering sight
Of the great garden, dense, entire
With fruit all year, and flying lizards
Settling in the tree of life,
Wings folded; and the sweet thorn-apple
Sharpening minds into a knife—
This land which none need go from, past
The distant, guardian sword of fire
That wavers to the left and right.

6

However vast and ancient are these
Epochs, all of them seem mirrored
In my temper, which can feel
Walled in, or else defenceless, eager
And thrusting like armies, soft as sand,
Cast down like cities; never still
But moving on to a new land
Or climate, all in a few hours—
Contracted yet exact, as after
Rain the storm-filled sky lours
In the smallest rut. But if

7[*]

There were an age yet earlier,
North of the dank Caucasian pass,
Before the everburning fields
And Tartarus the triple-moated

Town, and near the iron-throated
Mountain coughing brass and steel—
Then, as a woman, I have found
What we inherit in our blood,
From those bereaved by the first waste
And wailing for their menfolk drowned
In utter darkness of the flood.

While Satyrs Hunted for a Nymph

While satyrs hunted for a nymph
(We, for wild strawberries in a wood)
Philosophers, their blood and lymph
Excited by the search for Good,

Found Cause in Space; and tracked Despair
In Time; felt human Destiny
And Reason swaying in the air
Like a bee-tumbled peony;

Perceived (but never told their School)
Truth transparent as a shrimp
Darting backwards in a pool;
And Thought with all its tendons limp.

They are gone. Their counter-pleas
Of proof have left us, every one,
Like sailors whistling for a breeze—
And still the breeze drops with the sun.

Even So

In spite of striding
Lean-legged John's

Flaming words
In the wilderness;

And orators
Who stand in bronze,
Braving both
The rain and birds—

None the less,
Just as dogs
Prefer to lap
In filthy puddles,

So the fishwives'
Hands will chap,
Roofs fall loose
And walls get sick.

In spite of garlic
Breath of Rome
And senators;
In spite of lives

Good as a fable;
Envoys, tired
And fidgeting
At a treaty table—

Children still
Have pecked-out lungs;
The old maid slanders
All around;

Hope like a fox,
Has gone to ground;
And crowds feel hate
That burns their tongues.

Poisoned in Search of
the Medicine of Immortality

When Hsüang Tsung, great emperor,
Giddy and ill, carried in a litter,
Saw the stars sway,

His conquests and his arguments
And powers, falling into fever with him,
Pulsed their lives away.

Bow to his shade. To be at rest
Is but a dog that sighs and settles: better
The unrelenting day.

Epiphany in a Country Church

Rough-fisted winter and the blurred organ join
In minds of villagers to bring
A smell of wheatstraw under hoofs and sanfoin
In hay where beasts are fattening.

What does it matter if our wise men stress
The Barn as false, the Feast as wrong?
I hold the Magi were the wiser, yes,
To be believed in for so long.

A January mist now hides the wood;
Hard facts are overlaid by myth:
In us these last keep company, and should,
Like heart and bones in Farmer Smith

Who kneels to pray. Rubbing his neck—If beef
Goes up this month, he thinks . . . Round him
Confer vague consolations, powers of grief,
Man's fear and the high cherubim.

War and Peace

'Lately I cried with men.
Now once again
I wait for the slack of the tide,
Watch for a smooth in the wave and drop
My lobsterpots
Down between the grey rocks:
In the wet rope
Strong hope.

'The violence I was in,
Its crash and din
Are gone. My dear one, nothing breaks
When she holds it, or tumbles from her lap
Save when she starts up
Quickly to greet me or give me to sup:
In the folds of her dress
Gentleness.'

On Looking Down a Street

My mind's disturbed as rooks in the air . . .
May a thin-shouldered mountain hare
Or shy and meditative donkey,
Cat that gallops down an alley
And the squint-eyed, sandy dab,
Curlew, spider, vole and crab—
Creatures both severe and great
Or nimble as hens running under a gate—
Pray for me now. Lord, how I need
Their cleverness, their careful speed
Or power to be still, their sense,
Their pride and total innocence!
To keep from being fool or wretch
Till some hearse-horses trot this stretch.

Alter Ego

Mephisto and the Wandering Jew,
Ghost and gombie, witch and hoodoo:
    These are a tin cat-head
    Trembling on a thread
To frighten birds! The devil's brew
That does exist, stirs in you.

No malediction neared your crib;
Yet underneath the vaulted rib
    And flip-flap of your lungs,
    Darkly as in dung's
Warmth, there breeds and grows the glib
Cruelty that moves a nib,

Beats a dog, aims a gun,
Maims the Father, kills the Son,
    Infects a realm, and haunts
    The body with such taunts
And horrors that you shriek Be done . . .
I know, for you and I are one.

The Dog

1

Calm in their age, these city walls
Stand with full dignity at night,
Consoling men for what appals
And horrifies the waking sight.

2

Far down, low in the ditch, by stones
This urban power is founded on,
Some dog, sniffing for scraps or bones,
Feeling a sudden apprehension,

3

Yelps. And gathers answering yelp
And bark to reassure it. Oh
My soul, what can I do to help
Your guilt that lurks and runs below?

Funerals

Be done with show. Let the dead go to their lair
Unseen, a step barely heard on the stair.

A KITE'S DINNER

1954

The heart is a small thing, but desireth great matters.
It is not sufficient for a kite's dinner, yet the whole
world is not sufficient for it.

—ANON. 12th Cent.*

Everyman in the Wilderness

'Our own God travelled in his Ark
In step with us, by day, by dark.
The little landcrabs scuttled by
Like fears, transparent and too sly
For us to glimpse their homes. Our feet
Moved in scant grass; then manna, sweet
And trembling on the branch, was left
For boulders, shale and scree and cleft
Which, gasping, we yet had to climb . . .'
Such was their song. O cheating Time!
You will not, while the world unrolls
A curious design for souls,
Help those who have been glancing back
On old Egyptian wrongs and the black
Bruise of guilt for even longer
Than the Jews: you still defer
That green peace and the crops and sheep
Men see ahead and crave to keep.

A Tuscan Farmer

Why praise the huge past works of Hercules
When he leans idly on his club in Rome?
Come to my farm instead; walk round my home
When autumn puts its ladder in the trees
And what was stripped two thousand years ago
Is stripped again, or ploughed, made into stacks
And ricks and bundled heaps, by arms and backs
Aching with thrift. The least of plants that grow

As fodder have to fight the drought: my oxen,
Walking softly, pull with as great a strain.
Each clod, and hanging leaf, and wild grass cane
Is stronger than that strongest of all men
Whose lion, hydra, hell-dog, mares and boar
Were overcome indeed, but once, no more.

Lines for the Margin
of an Old Gospel

Children now awake to birds.
Mortals once rose to words
Fresh as the morning

When clover and the far hawks,
Scabious and meadow-larks
Shadowed a searing

That ran along nerve and sense
To mend a bad conscience
By caustic of loving.

Tax-collector and prostitute:
Perhaps they were astute,
More understanding

Than open throats, festered teeth,
Slovenly wits and breath
Gaping and crowding,

Or than any tolling-tongued
Masters who had wronged
Life with their learning.

Gently or fiercely, to all around
    He would explain, expound,
        Like a dog leaping

Through tall stalks of wheat:
    Such was the pounce and feat
        Of this debating;

Till an attic room rang
    With a sad air sung
        After the supping.

Destiny and darkness flow
    Faster, now, than low
        Clouds that are falling;

His friends snore, head to rock;
    The world takes stock,
        Hardly breathing.

Thinking how steepled jealousy,
    Prim-lipped authority,
        Pride of condemning

Can derive from that despair,
    Sleep, lantern, unfair
        Act of denying,

Warmth drains out of us. The soul
    Shown in its goodness, whole:
        No hammering

Of flesh to wood can harm that proof.
    Yet man is without roof
        And night is freezing.

Janus

1

A draught blown
Through January's door
Touches hard eyelids, chilled by night,
Of Two-Face, overseer
And guardian, who has always known
That warm and secret rite
Behind him, and the clear
Sharp light
Of any coming year.
Along this street, poor
Shutters, all thrown
Crookedly together, have their hinges closed
On shames, joys,
Longing, dread,
Restless and exposed
In dreams whose poise
Tilts back then leans ahead—
As if souls could explore
And fly in shuttlecock and battledore
Between life and the dead.
Till the town grumbles, clatters, gains its sight
And the last sleeper shakes,
Opens his mouth, wakes
And, jumping out of bed,
Uncombs the tangled morning noise.

2

And what if ships
Should break the distant skin of the sea?
Or plague or worm provide
Disaster for each olive-tree?
That is a last year's story
As today our lips
Forget rope, wind and tide,
Reasons and orders, while they speak

Of what we see:
A drop of water
Trembling in its slide
Along a sparrow's beak;
The blowsy girl who'll tweak
And laugh, pulling a little daughter
By her dress
Back to the old one's hips
Sunk down in massive happiness;
Or of a child who runs
With gutter treasure
To his mother while her face is like the sun's
Full pleasure
As her arms and knees
Jiggle the baby: fondness
Has no measure:
Newness no comparisons.

Venice Preserved

Under the tingling bongle-booming
Of St. Mark's, the pigeon-whirring,
Death-black shade and seablown hopes,
Light must dance and ripple. Copes
Of gold speak to the sun out loud
As crocus-mitres pierce a crowd
Policed where choirboys formulate
With shy and swaying, shuffling gait,
A ceremony old as dreams.*
O fond Evangelist: here gleams
His silvered, sleeping effigy
To dazzle hearts; then, dry and grey,
Skull and legbones under glass
Joggle at shoulder level, pass

Old men and Mickey Mouse balloons
While jew's-harps buzz and plainchant swoons
And postcard sellers, touts and pimps
Keep up their trade. A woman limps,
Pulls her black shawl, and with a tear,
Sees the slow walkers disappear,
Then puts thick fingers on her mouth
To kiss the whole warm, saintly South.

To lipping sounds of water, dark
As dissolution, we embark
Among these stones that weep in grandeur
For such hovels; for the slur
Of palaces whose bricks are cracked
From old decay or greed and racked
By ills; and for a poverty
That dreads a winter. Now, most gently,
We are shivering in moonlight
As if lovesick, while the night
Reveals each column, balustrade,
Dome and doorway. Unafraid
Of placards for some brand of gin
Where steamer-wash comes nosing in,
Or trash, or shabby songs: all merge,
Uplifted like a bridge's surge.
In her unbroken dignity
This trollop crumbles; painted, easy,
Filled with power to exploit
Prodigious charms and still adroit
In voice and beauty—she cajoles
Fine, votive answers from our souls.

Ease

By skilled pretence of conjuring one hour
    Of wholly unmolested power,
I call for noon prolonged. And let it be
    The summer of my days; agree
To flowering lindens where bees overflow;
    Or shade of currants, where I go;
Let seeding grasses touch my legs and nudge
    Their plumes: that Rhadamanthus, judge
And ruler in Elysian fields, may bless
    Such clear and easy happiness.

Rid of ambition—and the hope that fame
    Might one day mouth my whispered name—
I find delusion and her sighs in flight;
    Then gently as the sea at night
Breathes on a southern shore, the senses fall
    Assenting and forgiven. All
Who travelled home on hay-floats, warm and tired
    Will know my thoughts: this calm desired,
That gains sufficient strength to climb the steep
    Smooth orchard ladder into sleep.

Calendar

1

Too clean, the infant year, too new
And snowy innocent: it hides from view
Old rooted grudge and sin.

2

But memory floods to an edge
Of dark and bitter February sedge
That shivers like our skin,

3

And doubts are colder than the hands
Of men who harrow the long pasturelands
In painful discipline:

4

Until high mercy will assuage
The heart, and show it April's missal-page
Alive upon the ground.

5

Lovers now welcome thunderskies:
Their shock, the shelter, and a flash of eyes
That can be strange, profound,

6

Then tender as the fledgling days
Of June, when beauty trembles in the haze
With every rustling sound.

7

The halfway month. A pause for fears
Of middle-age, a deskful of arrears,
Time sped, so little done,

8

As heat lies heavy on the land.
Dogs snap at flies. Few tempers can withstand
The slowness of the sun,

9

Or parks that shrivel, leaves that spoil,
The sad allotments dug in a sour soil
Where towns and grime have won:

10

We need to feel gross sacks of grain
And in them, deities of earth and rain,
To put our sickness right.

11

The cake is crumbling, fires are lit.
Pink-pawed and back humped up, a mouse will sit
And nibble in quick fright;

12

And old, fat-fingered oaks are bare
While stars wheel through the empty, frozen air
To the slow hum of night.

The Hunter

Now show me any whole truth
Sustained as summer was in youth,
Plain and bare as winter trees,
Glittering like Ligurian seas,
Found in haycocks and in spires
Or lapping under hawser wires,
Burnt by meteor, scratched by fowl,
Alive in nudge and grin and scowl,
Proud as rags that sit alone,
Stronger than a dolmen stone,
As impertinent and wild
As a rough-haired tinker's child,
Sudden, like a gannet's dive,
Yet close and warm as honey-hive.

Because an old, obsidian face
Looks down in disillusioned grace;
Because, with pebbles spurting fear,
Siddhartha and his charioteer,
Fleeing through moonlight, found decay
And death and suffering on their way;
Because a half-wheel pulls a bell
And half a truth will serve to tell
Bewildered people; and a flash
Of dazzling knowledge gave one gash
To time when the great Doctor saw
His tomes, his tomes summed up as straw:
Shall I not ransack, search and tear
The clouds and grasses with my snare?

A Clerical Squire

Warm by the fire,
Toe in slipper,
Swinging his foot:
A clerical squire.
Where did he pass?
Outside, the Dipper
Ignores the spire.
Cold as brass,
Sour as soot,
Are death and desire.

THE LEAVES
DARKEN

1964

Darkness

And what will mitigate my life's long fault,
   I beg you, if authority's black stuffs
   Should fail to reconcile me
   To the final blindfold?
   Cassock and mortar-board
   Are under the same burden,
   Suffer the same problem, as ourselves;
   While conscience comes at night and stings
   The darkness: much as Carthage, ploughed under,
   Was then sown with salt.
A conjuror's cloak; the Queen of Spades
   With her poor migraine face: these
   Are for innocence: it waits agog,
   For flourishes of fireworks to exalt
   A pitchblack sky. Later,
   Incredible beliefs, the greatest things
   Given to the soul, are only
   Metaphors or hints
   Taken from lovers when they meet
   Bemused, in gardens,
   Among mooncast shadows
   Denser than a vault.
Let me predict my funeral weather
   Biting at black coats,
   With the new box—cave dark and cupboard thick—
   Brought to a lurching halt
   Near brambles and tipped headstones in the family
   Burial ground,* and flurryings
   Of shocked and interrupted jackdaws . . .
With so much still unlearned, ignored;
   So many moments of compassion skimped

By me or lost; this private graveyard seems
An apt memorial, with its church a ruin,
And its quiet cracked
By the quick clatter of black wings
In crude assault.

On Being of One's Time

1

Thistle lances are now broken
Through the winter woods, in a past tense
Of quarrels greenly spoken.
And the clock jerks on; each cog engaged,
Each weight, each wheel tied by obedience
And well caged.
That plain-faced clock whose stare
Is a big cheat,
Reminding me how eyes
Of men selling a horse will meet
One's glance in a fine honest glare
For the gigantic lies.

2

Keep step with tick and chime? But histories
In their divergence and entanglement
Force their own pulse to beat
Along my arteries,
Hobbling, racing ahead, or in retreat
From that odd ghost, the present.
Mountain among mountains, showing
Grey as its low raincloud overhead,
Mycenae lours
As if the murderous story were unsaid
And the warm air, at Aulis, waiting
In windless patience, knew the hours.

3

Am I committed purely to the moment?
No, with carved Hittite kings flaying

Prisoners alive (a thought abhorrent
As a fallout dread);
Fish-eaten Shelley rolling with the tide;
The twelvepenny dagger still in Marlowe's forehead;
Dying Keats watching the boatmen; and my nose twitching
From the flesh Spain burnt. Small wonder Zeno
And his arrow rused
Whole ages; while Plotinus, in a great stride
Of reason, fretted about Time: its flow,
And if what's at our throats, and gone, are fused.

Three Saints

Holy man in a mosque among roses and quails:*
Your sanctified floor two tigers each day
Come to brush with their tails,
Sweep with their tails.

Abu Zuláymah:* Arabian hills
Make you thirst for the coffee that green birds from Mecca
Have borne in their bills,
Carried far in their bills.

Juz Asáf of Kashmir,* do you come from a tomb
And torn-away linen: leaving us all
To find hope in our doom,
Your word, or vast doom?

Cartography
I

To map out man or woman,
Let your nervous hand try to lead
Wisdom by a twisted forelock.
Find what injuries were done
To self-esteem: redress
The boundary; give fads attention.

Measure out loneliness.
If you hold the plan
Still workable, think how a weathercock
Will rule an empty street at night;
Or that a smudge of print can cite
Those full extravagancies
Waiting in a grub; or plant-seed;
Or the mind—
Wild as equinoctial seas—
Of ordinary humankind.

2

A boat slewed
Towards the urgent flood,
Its anchor fluke dragging mud
And cable fouled: that goes for most of us. We risk
Mishandling time, whose hurry
Carries off branch, bole, root, in spate.
I've watched rank pulled away, near tamarisk
And the Bermudian tides, where a proconsul made
Gestures too old and negligent;
And there, known a massive brain prematurely
Crumble in wrecker's dust;
Learnt how young sailors dropped, beside a carronade
And hulk, on sand: no moment
Being right or just.
While coral of praise or gratitude
(You've guessed) can come too late.

3

Does this smack
Overmuch of water? But one's
Life can be a voyage
To Cythera: in black
Storms; faint calm; or else uneasy from cross-currents
Of what's difficult or fluent.
As there's no finish to our quirks, beliefs,
Distorted theories and failing reasons,
We might embark

For coasts that wear a greener plume,
Where caverns rest the mind in dark,
Leaving a crystal-shattered spume
Outside. No light can gauge
Hollows and sudden gaps, or chart
Those devious reefs
And unsure soundings of one person's heart.

Patriarchs

1

Debenture holder of great flocks and folk,
Lavish Abraham, the undefeated:
    Jacob your grandson wrestles.
    Nerve and gut and sinew
Push with the sap of Sarah: she whose cockled face knew
Every patriarchal ploy of yours; each joke;
    And loved your lies; looked mild;
    But laughed when unexpected
Callers ate under terebinths, on trestles,
To foretell her real, her wriggling child.

2

This night is starless, quiet. Just a heave,
A grunt, a change of hold, and shuffling feet.
    'Only one system, one true
    Method—and that's guile,'
Says Jacob to himself with a quick con man smile.
'Whom need one fight but God? Others I can deceive.'
    The angel sobs, quite lost,
    Begging his freedom with sweet
Promises; till Jacob, hip askew,
Limps off at dawn; as always, at light cost.

3

Grandsire, your noble new idea, grown old,
Longed for Machpélah's cave. Charred in an urn,
    Your spine can rest. Your views,
    Distant as Isaac's aim

Or Jacob's catchy wits, prove that although a prince came
Poorly dressed, who knew that all should suffer and told
    Men to love—so pricked
    Are we and blessed in turn,
  We live as if not knowing the Good News,
  Expediently, still cheating and still tricked.

Continuity

When morning came lightly as a hare's breath,
      Worry held us
      In its copper snare
    With a sick pull of death.
      We were alone
Under the anger of old people and their
    Bias. Now, walking crookedly,
      We're mottle-red;
      Shrunk or paunchy;
Brittle as curled-up leaves; or rancorous;
      Others ghastly,
      Like a bone:
Fearing our sons and their bold, brilliant stare.

Youth and Age

I

Comfort is small as a snipe's heart to a child,
    The world suspect,
  And laughter a snickering of knives.
This boy, with hair curled tight as any faint, distant
    Forest of hung tapestry,
Has thoughts that quickly dip and rise like finches in flight.
    No pedant, no burnt pod
Of learning, can deflect him while he moves
    Apart, in a thin
  Simple air, hardy as a saint,
    With the same triumph.

Mountain mists both frenzy and suffuse him,
Till they melt
Into vast torpor, a bored dream.
He might—as Bruce's heart in a box was thrown into battle—
Offer his adored a rose,
Alone, in a closed garden and with trembling knees.
Such youthful Lists of Love,
Which become jest and rage and bullying,
Can make him use
The extreme and hermit right to pray and fast,
Ignored, on rocks.

3

Oaths of yesterday are stale, sickly
As hawthorn smell.
Big in his strength, he'll stride bare hills,
Then ripening lowlands, to where dykes, ports and tides
Control the State, commerce, one's life.
Honesty may turn or quit; argument's useless.
He must learn to rig
His balance-pans of pride and skill, and make
The debit less,
The honour large: liking to take or give
With mastery.

4

So cool the summer and so dulled the fair,
He sits, afraid,
Under his armorial tree
While its dry branches creak and rattle like a relic
Of his anger as he shakes
A stick. Veins knot, and arteries are choked, to know
The years so burdensome
Or else too light, too null. Those sly and laughing
Children who played
Near have run: they're gone from his weak sight
And feebler tears.

For My Dead Friends

Fit for a knacker's yard,
This carcase of a poor
Parthenon, purged and marred,
Is such a prodigy
None can feel condescending. From its floor,
Where wagtails run and dip
In marble puddles after morning rain,
Columns empower the air with flesh,
Not stone, tender and fresh:
Making a pain
Of exultation grip
The midriff-soul with love.
Where to turn, giddy from shock?
Below, a woman spins, shouts to a neighbour;
Children play. High, high above,
Sea-eagles, circling slowly, eye with disfavour
Any shell left chipped and empty
On a rock.

So, harassed puny man
Has built, ennobling the weak moment.
Taking stock, we can
Jot down that in no matter what ironic
Landscape people work and die—
The serious, foolish, modest, lewd,
The bold or shy, violent or subdued,
With their diversity of features,
Humours, failures—
They have renewed
Their pity and are found
Forgiving God each tragic,
Tearing thing,
Throat swollen and voice faltering
From gratitude.
What more should I,

Muddled and earthbound,
Need for the soul's nourishment?

3

In spite of which I waste
My breath, and spill live sorrow on the thought
That we, who carry friends
Like a good taste
In the mouth, so short a time, ought
To be left, not random odds and ends
For a remembrance, not a shard
Stupidly small and hard,
But an emphatic plier
That can wrench the mind, turn it and amaze;
Some elegiac force
Whose lunge and potency
Could lather Phaethon's reins, each horse
Sun-bent though undisastrously:
More than Achilles felt when mountain flanks
Showed muletracks, scarred all sideways,
To get planks
To feed Patroclus' fire.

4

The pen scratches and flies drone
And towns suffer heat,
And I know life can be weariness
And the sour pleasure of the incomplete.
To ease it calls for metaphor.
I'll take, then, for my own
Hand, the Parthenon, that hollowness
Above new Athens, quite distinct
From the complexity
Spread out beneath, but linked
With every roof and hearth, as what is true
Should be; that shell
Now flushed by haze, colour of asphodel*—
And pick it up, and hold it to my ear
Whenever, privately, I wish to hear

Its murmur celebrate
Those whom I knew
Who were both good and great.

A Query

Rusted, small, weed-hidden
And unlocked, forgotten:
Such was the backdoor
Of the unbelievable Byzantine citadel.
So when Turks elbowed through it, grunting, to dispel
This blaze unseen before—
A jewel-hung emperor as Christ Pantokrator—
Who were the faithful, who the infidel?
Experts are cunning and say nothing more.

On Reading What Happened
after Noah

Float! Cast off the rope!
It has grown dark.
Poor talk, small hope,
Mix with the stench of the Ark.

The keel grounds. A new air
In nameless trees:
After one breath, one stare,
We pray, drink, curse and seize.

Come back, you morning of fresh
Leaf and slope,
Gleam on our flesh
With your effulgent scope.

But no. Savage, forlorn,
We need to be
Inked in with thorn
And gall, for clarity.

When Moore Field Was All Grazed

When Moore field was all grazed
And Finnesburie ploughed,
People were fiery, clever, glum or crazed;
Hard knuckled; and proud
Liars; and well-phrased.

God's Nature, A Guessing Game

*Tinker**

Proud as a Paleologue, whose ninety
Thousand frying pans
His forbears had to patch,
This rogue stares

Full at my eyes, aloof, in scorn.
Rags and raindrops catch
In the hedge, to show his kind
Despise and hate

Roof or chair or chimney cowl,
But need to share some narrow
Edge with slug and beetle,
Thorn and frog.

His blunt-nosed women, heavy shawled
And still as stones, gaze

At their whippet bitch that trembles,
Lame. Why then

Have fear and shame crawled up my bones,
Until he turns to crack
Twigs and get the sopping
Ditch ablaze?

Tailor

Crouchback, with a crunch of scissors,
On a bare, hard floor,
He fills his mind with shadows.
Some are kind

As the old whispering leaves of Mamre;
Some could fold behind
A door in ghettos; others
Are charred years

Of being outcast; tears; and a vast
Final heap that wastes
And heaves at Dachau, nearly
Dead. "Judge not . . .*

"Be a lover of peace, a maker of peace . . ."
He bastes a thread. Back bent,
It must not tire. And Hillel
Also said:

"In my abasement is exaltation."
The tailor lifts his eyes.
All pain is black: they glow,
They run with fire.

Soldier

Time's a thief; and terror comes
By mouthfuls, with a roar
Of drums; until a bleat
Of musketry

Makes Grief go hooded down the street
And Hunger tug her shawl.
The soldier: did he shiver
When he gained,

Then spilled, the tumbling walls of fortress
Tiryns—(only magpies,
Now, and milk-veined thistles
Warm its heart)—

Or wrenched Jerusalem apart?
He'll cackle in the pub, tell
Lies, and rub a stiffness
Of the knees.

His children play at marbles, or they
Sing: 'We won't surrender,
We won't surrender, you king
Of the Barbarees.'

Sailor

In a dream of dolphin calm,
He can feel monsters gleam
And maul, deep under bow
And keel; and crabs

Slide to the turn and fall of tide,
Where caves weep, and rocks
Burn, and oceans glint
Like silverfoil.

Now for the dogwatch mandolin,
With tunes of sunset, home
And tears: the sailor's debt
To all his dears,

Before a strong shuddering lurch and foam
Through which his vessel raves
And slats; till hawsers pull
At quays that hint

Complexity, flaw, unease,
In black winds along wharfs
Where stocks of goods spoil
And rats gnaw.

Rich Man

He jokes and humphs with dignities
Of robes, smoothness of jaws,
Huge shade of palaces
And strength of laws;

While tongues of lie and gossip guess
His powers, where they reach
And how they're swayed. Now
He provokes despair,

Now showers gold. His gardeners, high
On rungs, who pleach and clip,
Hold his commands to mean
There should be nothing

To reproach in green, or to
Confute in gilt. Fountains,
Gates, are filled by crowds,
Shuffling and mute;

While rivergods, who had to turn
To figured stone, are blind
To weed and spotted loach,
And tilt their urn.

Poor Man

Mistrust, by a small cough, betrays
Its loneliness, as through
The dusk, a frightened tap
Of heels hurries

Past crimes a gate or privet hedge
Or curtain-net conceals.
Days are a slap in the mouth,
A kick in the crutch,

From citizens so virtuous,
Suburban and polite,
They'd hate to touch this creature
Who'll pick up

Fag ends from gutters, with no mind
To work or please or care.
Let their souls rot (he mutters
As he bends)

For being unaware of seas
That lie behind the brimming
Tears and red-net eyeballs
Of a sot.

Beggarman

Grincing on a yellow fiddle
In a town where gulls
And grime mix in the air's
Familiar chime

For priest and bookie, Dooley's Bar,
Swans and sticks and dead old
Buckets on the Liffey
Mud—he knows

Men turn their head away when walking
Past, and flush in the cold,
As if their breath or blood
Had a catarrh

So vehement, it made them choke
To brush against the Four Last
Things of death, judgement,
Heaven and hell.

For who of us can tell what pride
Or freedom may yet croak
For pennies on the windy,
Wet kerbside?

Thief

No footfall. Not a squeak of a hinge.
But midnight is stabbed;
The core of the house prised
And grabbed. Weak

And sore, you feel hands have fumbled
Your heart's cage. Then, when

He's caught, you rage. All this
He understands.

And now his way is to indict.
He'll think that you, fool owner,
Are wrong. Not he, such a poor-
Looking, gaunt crook.

Let a strong list of saints, or device
Of fans vaulting an apse,
Cool the smart and taunt
Of his look, which says:

'Perhaps you forget. My counterpart
Was set up to fulfil
A prophecy, was promised
Paradise.'

Hermes, Protector of Landmarks and Travellers

Runnels trickle through course grass;
No one is near this cairn of stones.
Throwing another on
(A Mayo hilltop needs old ways)
I feel most private, moved and proud
When the wind cuffs me as you pass.

The Leaves Darken

If a child's tale were sung
To kings and the tired spearmen;
Or if Outer Isles, fog-blind,
Are found only by raven

Croaks; or a new housing scheme should geld
Some king-cup creek;
If Menelaus hung
His head in Egypt
After war was done,
While gnats, then flies, sipped
His blood by night and blistering sun
Until those bony temples held
Ideas that were quite brittle, hollow, weak;
As an old parrot tears a rind
From sugary belief—
So, juices of the year
Dry into blacker leaf
And darker fear.

The Foxy Smell of Fear

I

The foxy smell of fear
    Can change, by a sharp catch of liking,
    Into prim, clear
    Morning snuff, clean as November's
    Bracken after frost.
    And spice-leaves, bruised by blunderers
    In the warm dark, where tree-frogs sing
    Like bells on a lost
    Troika trace,
    Are altered and enhanced. Hymettus,
    No. Its honeycombs,
    Paper-thin, are ghostly homes
    Of men whose buzz was disputatious
    In the market-place.
    Up the road, cowled in mist,
    St. John the Hunter's Church may stare
    Over all Athens; and with Attic flair
    For moments like Clean Monday, can insist
    You bite the sea

Itself and gulp, cold and quick—
Urchin and octopus from the Saronic
Gulf—in true hyperbole.

2

Fisherboys are stretched asleep
On the seawall of Alexandria.
Travel, move further on. Then keep
Forever in your skull
That peppered scent
Of Africa, from the acacia
And dried grasses. Back at home,
Brewers' vats, seething
Black in their digestion, may annul
The sour and filthy smell
Of railway fumes
Which hang near clinkers of embankment
Slopes, where desperations of poverty
Once used to roam
And bindweed has tried living.
Better invoke
The hag at Delphi.
High Parnassian spell
Or not, kings taken aback
(So one assumes)
Or garlanded: power lay in a floor whose stonecrack
Let out laurel smoke.

Village Seasons

A gauzewing fly lights on my hand;
Birds echo; wildest promises abound
And hawthorn creams the land.

Summer, lazing on her elbow,
Watches unremitting mowers, thirsty,
Dazed, work to and fro.

123

Gold coins—a fortune—drop from trees
Into ditch-coffers underneath the ash
That dangles rusty keys.

Now pumps wear topknots made of straw
And roads clang underfoot; young cheeks shine red,
Bright as a hedge haw.

But cottage Death, huge fisted, wrings
The sheet out when it pleases her, intent,
Intent on other things.

With Palate for Fine Things
but Penny Mouth

1

With palate for fine things but penny mouth,
I have to tell what sourness, drouth,
Juice, or sweet, lodges in the core
Of those I learn from, groan with, like, or else deplore.
Seldom I feel—left on a tooth—
Wisdom's honey or the wax of truth.

2

Man, this bag of blood, a battlefield
Of civil war, in turn must yield
To his own cowardly and parched tongue,
Then to heroic blaring of a trumpet lung;
Now to disgust, now awe: his soul
Feeling God's shoulder working in the mole.

3

A painted fable, endlessly begun,
Of lovers in a varnished sun
Is often craved. Instead, the rain
Stutters and beats all night against the window pane,

And grates get cold and tenebrous,
While a child dies like picked convolvulus;

4

And pride, for persons of whatever stock;
Or promptings of revenge; or shock
Are ready, instantly, to rip a heart
Out that a silly tea-leaf tale may play its part
Or myth be acted. Statues are set
Up, and plaques: then English crowds forget.

5

Nine chains, unseen, hobble St. Peter's dome,
Or it would hurl apart. Is Rome
So different from mortal brain and skull?
Tabu and geas,* dogma and veto can annul
Some of our copious projects, deeds,
And ruses. But, below the varied Creeds,

6

Are woods unhunted by Hippolytus,
Sea floors unsucked by Proteus.
In time, all trees will echo;
Swaying corals will rear up to grow
Inside a crested wave that must advance
And roar its words against our ignorance.

7

If these same messages (carried by weathers
And the winds, as if in feathers
Of warm birds that find their way
Between the Cape or Horn, Faroes or Thunder Bay)
Could be endearing, yes. But hardly one
Holds promise: only desperation;

8

Insolence; courage of the clan;
Or that historic yell of man
With a new bludgeon. After tremendous fire,
Will there be any haybarn, bookshelf, pavement, spire:
Or only a small pock and rise
And suck of mangrove mud for insect eyes?

9

Head low, old folk, old horses; but head high
The young. When children crane and pry
For nests, twig-dust and darkness fall in
Their eyelids while they part dense branches. Trust the thin
Necks and wrists: feel safe from doom.
Think. Lazarus stepped freely from his tomb.

Miniature Paean

1

When porpoises played to each creaking
Of a clinkered boat and round
The vine-mast Dionysus found,
Men would line their cheeks from seeking
What can free, exalt, astound;
More were holding back their bile.
The rest, perhaps, could reconcile
Their gods with the hard, mattocked ground.

2

But now, to feel as proud or blest
As the past kings of Vizapore,
Elect in rubies, rich from bézoar,*
We must hear ourselves confessed
Because, regardless, we implore
Some power to force the larks to wake,
To keep seas shimmering, and shake
Our own wits sharply, peel and core.

3

However grey Mycenae looks,
The Argive plain gleams ahead,
Golden as Aegisthus' tread;
While, sleepless, travelling in books,
I follow where great names have spread.
A goods train grumbles through the dark;
Soon, quite near, a fox will bark.
Vixen warmth makes a fine bed.

Dusty nettles by a farm
Smell good to those who step ashore,
Tired out by the sea's hurt and uproar.
With the last grain-sack safe from harm,
Hauled up to lofts, how fine to pour
One's body into freshly tucked
And laundered peace. I've found and sucked
What nourishes, what can restore;

5

Though my stupidity's been grief
Since I have grown from chin to toe.
And yet the cornucopias flow
With music, sea-wrack, insect, leaf,
Well-set page of folio,
Banded snail-shell—for delight,
Awe, pain, ease and fright—
To the mind's high vertigo.

Cameo

Amalfi's poverty
Swelled to an Archbishopric
After that wrong-hour clang and topple of its shaky,
Meagre belfry,
After wounds and cries in sulphurous panic.
Earth lay fat at last, rich, heavy
From volcanic
Terror: and no crone need any
Longer claw up a stick.
In contrast, rosemary
Or scrub grow thick
Beside the Appian Way; and who can see
Much more than sheep, quick
And thin, gobbling dry fennel hungrily,
Where Hadrian's prospect used to be?

Adam

Poor Adam! Marrying
A screech-owl* before Eve was made
And liable to meet God walking
Slowly, in the humid, dusky glade.

Sonnet

I'll speak of Alexander's honied corpse;
Or Arthur's well-gashed skull, with one dint raw
The day they buried him; what Phaedra saw
From behind leaves: for these are fibres, warps
And chains connecting every creature's soul
Inside humanity; never outdated,
But as horrible as streets of slated
House-rows in Victorian grime and role
Of industry, which had no Artemis:
Only an upright piano and the hymns.
I'll speak of these, then ask: When heads or limbs
Are lopped in private hate and war, is this
More terrible in hills, or where men mow,
Or Mons, or Troy, or mound of Jericho?

An Answer from Delphi

I

To keep a balance and to bear
The world; its disarray;
Its wounds; its many failures
Of attempts to supplicate untold
Divergencies of gods angry or gay,
Innocent or shrewd
By souls a hotch-potch of what's bold,
Eager, alarmed, submissive, wily, crude—
We know such warring humours
Have to be resolved. But where?

Beneath a gold mosaic, spanned
By plainchant, resonant with praise
And punishment? Or in
Aeolian islands, ridden by winds, by brightness,
The Bermudas, when a conch shell brays?*
Where sages struck a chill
In Ireland's side, through hound, princess
And cattle-thieves, with a strong, holy quill?
Under the salt and skin
Of Jutish estuary land?

3

Parnassos and its rocks resound
With cries of little birds,
Diminished priests of Apollo.
Poverty must work to mule-bells and the clear
Water's tumble. No Castalian words
Are needed to contain
One riddle by another: here,
Sacred and common are conjoined and plain,
While feathery tremors grow
From olive trees clenched in the ground.

Warning

To be content, you furrow-faced ones, who have a temper
    Stinging as radishes,
    Hot as boiled onion,
    Rough as brown bread;
    Relishing the first Isaiah naked,
Preacher of the jostled street—
    Moralists, pruned too far
    Back, punished,
    All but finished:
Keep out of boyhood
    Lanes your legs once dawdled in,
    or skipped along.

Common Wish

Love plays in the sun,
Sickens, droops and is done.
A spider's thread
Rolls up, binds up her dead.
There is too much
For us between a dockleaf's touch
And Saturn, which with frosty rings
In utter darkness whirls and stings.

Gleam candour, friend,
Blush to the very end,
Alert and quick
And warm as a hind's lick
Over her calf
To comfort it. Keep near. Then half,
A third, the whole of us could choose
To sop, not crack, our mortal bruise.

HER STORMS

1974

Behold, the world is full of trouble, yet beloved: what if it were a pleasing world? how would'st thou delight in her calms, that canst so well endure her storms?

—St. Augustine
taken from Quarles's *Emblems*

Glastonbury

Pilgrims to Glastonbury
Marvel at its holy thorn,
Cratagaeus praecox, and are moved
By echoes given
From Joseph of Arimathaea.

A kindly legend born
Of magic calls for love;
Being deep-rooted as a simple,
Blessed as bread, dependable
As are downs and their dewponds:
It needs respect from both
The pious and the unshriven.

Clonmacnois*

Along the gently
Sloping riverbanks
Of Shannon with its placid flow
And all its wildfowl,
Why should the ruins
Of Clonmacnois,
Pillaged by savages
When most renowned and holy—
Why do its ravages,
In fact,
Make the heart easy
With high calm, tact
And harmony?

Man and Beast

Carefully
The Celtic warrior held his right arm,
His sword arm,
Out of the baptismal water,
Like Lord Macartney
Refusing to kowtow to an emperor—
Even the great Ch'ien Lung.

Mistrust and dignity
And puissance have more
Beauty when a lion,
Eagle or big cobra
Wishes to be arrogant.

Not Forgetting Aeneas Sylvius

Not forgetting Aeneas Sylvius—
Novella writer and then Pius the Second—
Gloriously borne aloft
Into the Lateran's basilica
To face a sacristan who knelt
Holding a wisp of burning cotton on a pea-stick:
Totter-man, or throne, needs a reminder
Of how short is triumph,
How it never condescends.

Tyranny

Antigone's no rebel:
She must fulfil
The ancient rite.
She cannot leave
Her brother to the kites.

In spite of Creon, walling-up
And death by hanging, she
Did manage—just—to put
Some small earth over him.
Before dogs found the body.

History lacks a Teiresias
To speak our future.

How then to fend off tyrants?
Proteus in sea-caves,
Old Proteus, will not say
Although he knows;
But glides into an undertow,
Flits over sand, or flows
Beneath the pride
And camber
Of a wave, hiding
From questioners.

Cheiron

Cheiron the wise Centaur
(So the tale went)
Tutored Achilles, Jason
And Asklepios in how to shoot
A bow, in music,
And all magic that he knew
Of herbs and medicine.

A school that let you race
Against the clouds,
Or lie on cushions of spice-odoured plants,
Or make a lyre-string
Tremble and echo round a cave,
In true Arcadia—one without a skull:

Wild honey on the tongue
To think of for a moment!
Bitter the next,
From knowing it a myth.

Carpaccio

St. Ursula dreaming
And the little dog guarding her
Neither are disturbed
By that gentle
Angel of death who opens the door
Quietly

Then on a day
That has each pennant flapping
She embarks on the green sea of Venice
To be martyred in Cologne
Her host of companions
Killed with her

Eleven thousand virgins
Or so it goes
Totally absurd you think
But what a pinprick beside
Each fatuous intake
Of each common breath

Brigid

Brigid, once
Protector of poets;

Patron of Kildare
Where nowadays foxhounds

Keep muzzles down to the scent
While bullocks fatten;

Worshipped by Romans
Under Severus in York;

Protector from domestic fires
In Ireland
And now its own saint;

Lady, I bow to your diversity.

St. Francis

St. Francis when he lay blinded
Hated mice.
They ran off with his bread.
Never would he laud them
Or call them brother.

With his eyes cured
There were the birds of course
Also bed-bugs and fleas
And pebbles on the road
Lodging in his sandals
To preach to
And profess his love for.

But not one good word
Did he have
For the wise and patient
Overloaded donkeys
Red with sores
And bruised by sticks
That he met
On the long way to Rome
And back.

Murex

1

Cleopatra the Greek-lipped . . .
Great Alexander gave our country
   To his general.
Pure Macedonian-bred, these Ptolemies
Who've held this Egypt for three hundred years
Or, if you'd sooner, twelve generations
   Of a ruling sister
Married to a brother, as compelled
By Pharaonic, strong official habit.

2

Brilliant and at ease, sure,
   Shrewd in governing
The upper and the lower land whose tongue
She's first of her long line to speak—
   Her might, even her magic,
Stream from innate good heart and head.
   Carried among us
She can understand, she hears: brave queen.
   Fit daughter of the sun-god Rê.

3

She has commanded a shore mollusc
   (From a grey sea-shell)
Crushed by the ton, to give a juice
   So pale, so clear, it shows no colour.
In dim work-lofts, men who steep a stiff
   Fine-woven cotton in deep troughs
Of it, and know the art, have found this stuff,
   If nursed away from light,
Seems as if soaked in water, nothing else.

4

Daybreak, and I pressed near when a huge sail
   Was dragged on to open ground.
   The sun glanced,
   Then like a young lover
   Gazed on it till it blushed

Into astounded purple.
This was to live—to grow as at a trumpet-yell
   Of valour. Then a hymn
Was sung. My chest still feels the ache.

Ocean Through a Mask

And the fishes of the sea shall declare unto thee . . .

What seraphim could dance
More curiously than these—
More brilliant than jewels—
With shiver of fins
And wings that tremble?
Or what gold-leafed cherubim could look
More languid and more radiant
Guarding a coral reef
That is the tabernacle
Of their life?

Fifty Years Past

Fifty years past, but it stays sharp:

This splinter of land,
Cone-seed of history.

Between humped rocks of Nazareth
Comes bleating at night
And fires that blink from goatskin tents.
Magdala a tattered village with fowls.

Near Jaffa, the wind is brilliantly alert
With meadowlarks and hawks
As it sweeps over downs,
Carrying salt that rusted the crusading armour
But now bends marguerites and scabious.

A camel goes wild in a cloverfield,
Throwing off its load bit by bit,
The small boy who'd led it
Standing rooted.

And a gazelle crossed the empty plain
Of Samaria, the light fading.

How can one forget?

The Fetch-Light

Known as a fetch-light
And omen of death,
A gleam floating
Through the winter night
Over some rooftop,
Tillage, copse or park,
Was only a harmless owl gliding
With its feathers luminescent
From a rotted stump.

I crave one small
Owl-coin of Athens
To hold against
Calamities, or just the dark.

Hope

Hope or so I fancy
Is bright-haired
And nimble

Tufts of seapinks
Come up in her footprints
And where her fingers
Touch a wall

Heart's-ease grows
From the crevice

If she pauses a moment
In a family graveyard
Then blue bugle
Will cover the ground

For all her youth
She is old as humanity
And none else
Long ago
Could have refreshed the soul
In shadowy
Deep-layered Lebanon

War and blight
All known miseries
Yap at her heels

But she keeps ahead

Pitchforks

Pitchforks tossing the dead
Like mice in stable straw,
So people thought,
Had prongs that went through
Gullet and heart.

I know Hell is to feel
A mother's son,
The white-necked boy,
Grown and pointing those tines
To pierce my head
Then rip me apart.

A Question

They fly back to their hives*
To feed each other honey—
Bees already aswarm—
If you bang kettles or pans
As Virgil clanged a pair of cymbals.

Is there a pitch of sound or clatter
That will alter dreams
From what's disturbed and densely black
To such sweet succour?

Blinded Bird Singing

This blinded bird singing,
What can he think about,
Pinioned by a cage? God's grief,
How can he sing? Without
Miltonic,* high extravagance
Of learning, still
He exults, hailing
The holy light
As if each quill
Could feel its way between
A branch and leaf
Where tree-wasps dance
And grubs are found
Under the bark
By a keen
Prising bill,
And every thicket seen
Has its own multitudes of sound,
And night—true night
Is never still,
Never such total dark.

One's Due

Wife-beaters of course and constant liars,
The delicately mean or wilfully feeble,
People bent on provoking a child's scream
Or its future downfall,
Those sick with envy
And the high boasters,
Merit that burning rubbish-dump
Of stinking corpses, sewage and offal
In the long ditch running below Jerusalem,
Known as Ge-Hinnom.

I should be there
For a heap of quiet crimes:
Chances of good aborted
When my tongue was too quick
Or my heart too slow,
The lost moment,
Unmeant betrayals from sheer
Inadvertence or stupidity—
Huge or trifling,
These too call for the pit.

Back

The dark-breasted flesh of a swan
Needing much blood to beat its great wings
How fiercely I wish it would
Carry me

Not away from death
In whose fist I've been held
Too often to be afraid
Of the last clenching

Nor towards that vigour of passion
Where fate speaks directly
To each person in a marble theatre
Perhaps at Epidavros
And gods and goddesses are vengeful or petulant
Bullying us then
As now

But back
          to those pleasant places
Where surprise was quick as nettle-stings
And amazement blushed from the dog-rose
And somewhere in the hedge was a little
Uptailed wren.

That Altar to Pity

That altar to Pity
Which Pausanias saw;

St. Eustache à la chasse
In Chartres sparing
One holy stag;

The Holly and the Ivy sung
By fresh-faced nurses
Through each ward;

They all close my throat.

But the nine rivers of hell
Leave me untouched
Because their sources escape me,
Except when I walk
Over the dark
Bogland of Roscommon.

View

At the sea's edge, near Bray
In County Wicklow,
From a lonely
Field for dumping rubbish,
Water and air seemed shining, pearly,
Still. No sound.
Gulls rode the gentlest swell
Of this small estuary.

Nearby in Rocky Valley
Among small concrete homes
Fenced round with wire,
One could smell
Bracken and a few sheep, and see
Both copper domes of Powerscourt
Rising over the haze, far off.
Domes and domesticity, entire
As stallions, but now
Burnt to the ground.

On Seeing the Pleiades Rise

Toes among sharp blades
In a male sword dance:
Not to be tried by women
Or its meaning is lost.
And a hen blackbird
Before she mates,
Trailing her wings
To make them brush slowly
Along the ground.

I need to think about
These, and related things,

Anew. But the mind is bound
By habit and morals,
And I might be a Dyak waiting
To plant his rice at the proper
Moment, which is
On seeing the Pleiades rise
Just before dawn.

A Melancholy Love

Part elegant and partly slum,
Skies cleaned by rain,
Plum-blue hills for a background:
Dublin, of course.
The only city that has lodged
Sadly in my bones.

In a Dublin Museum

No clue
About the use or name
Of these few
Bronze Age things,
Rare
And in gold,
Too wide for finger-rings.
Till some old epic came
To light, which told
Of a king's
Daughter: how she slid them on to hold
The tail ends of her plaited hair.

ADMISSIONS

1977

Waking

When Lazarus
Was helped from his cold tomb
Into air cut by bird-calls,
While a branch swayed
And the ground felt unsteady:
I must, like him, with all force possible
Try out my tongue again.

Admissions

Let us then freely admit
That any windfall fruit
May have a wasp in it;

That to hear the word 'fox'
Or see one, prevents an Aran
Fisher putting out;

That Seville's bearers of Passion
Figures, drunk, can shout:
'Your Virgin's a whore!'

That Jachin and Boaz, bronze
Pillars of endurance and might,
Fell with the Temple.

Any Weekday in a Small Irish Town

A rusty, nagging morning.
By the pub's
Front door, now shut,
An ass-cart waits and waits.
This scrap of donkey
Wearing blinkers cracked, old,
Askew, blocking one eye,
Has also a string
Bridle pulled on crookedly
And tight enough to smother:
You can see where it rubs.

At dusk, cornerboys
So shy
And full of silent hates,
Get lanced by rain and cold.
They stand beside
The factory gates
Before the shift goes off,
Scowling at each other.
Girls hurry out
Together, giggling by.
And still the donkey waits.

Mycenae

You double lioness of Mycenae
Rearing up each side
Of the male pillar:
Must you guard this gate
To keep alive
The high citadel and the whole story?

Taking fallen rocks
Then adding blood, muscle and flesh
To bones, putting in stomach and heart—
An old man wintering alone
Or the usual peasant nurse
Willing to spin tales,
Could tell it.

Perhaps a criminal record
Neatly typed
In a police file somewhere
Holds a comparable event.

But goat-bells on the very spot
Clink out:
This is not so.
Clouds leaning darkly on these mountains,
And the Argive plain, always sunlit,
Equally affirm
That ancestors of Agamemnon
Breathed this air. His family,
Cursed by Pelops,
Made its love and murders
Occupy us now
So that our napes bristle.

Dark Romney Marsh

Dark Romney Marsh,
Its air filled
With sheep-smell and skylarks,
Riverscent, bleating.

That black pebble*
In the Hebrides,

Well known as an oracle
And needing certain
Formalities of approach.

Lucent or silvery
Grey bream, snapper and mullet,
Feeding in shallows
Of a warm sea.

Yunnan, enfolded by cloud
On other clouds, where they say dogs
Bark at the sun.

The half-seen; a shadowy
Statement: these can be
More subtle
Than a vivid declaration,
More enticing.

Remote Matters

As long as I can kneel to tell
Pin-eyed from thrum-eyed primroses
Or find a small cranesbill
In rough grass,
Why should I mind
If Dunwich is under the sea
With nine churches drowned?

The Heavenly Twins

Give me those horse tamers,
Castor and Pollux,
Under whose sign I was born—

Not on account of false
Clues that glint out
From the zodiac—

But merely for the feel
Of softest muzzle
Allied to much force;

The smell of leather; a clean
Curb-chain to finger
Or a plain belly-band.

These twins who chipped the shell
Of Leda's eggs
Have yet more fame: in tempesty

Weather (Brixham talk)
They'd quell the waves.
Dioscuri, I love you.

Ilex

Ilex: all shadows
Belong to your tree.

Your forbears grew
Beside high terror
Felt by Greeks
Also near Roman treachery.

The sacred oaks of Mamre
Known to Abraham
Rustled their leaves
In prophecy,
But ilex:
Yours rattle drily

As if from little fears
And doubts continually
Moving, hidden
In your dark centre

Or from some shame
That we recall
Painfully
In the night.

Vanessa Cardui, butterfly

What human beauties
Pocket Venuses
Can match *Vanessa*

'Painted Lady'
Fragile
Exquisitely veined

Leaving North
Africa to reach
Ireland

With flirting
Delicate flutter
Of iron obstinacy

Bird

Plummeting
Suddenly
In Hebridean seas,
A gannet.

Dropping
A snail to hit
A rock and crack its shell,
A thrush.

Piercing
A muddled head,
The glint from a bright wing
Of thought.

Shredding
An open heart
With crook'd and dirty talons,
Betrayal.

Sparrow

Slim, chic and pale,
This young sparrow looks, pecks, looks.
His beak and my thumbnail
Are made of the same stuff,
Spin with the same atoms.
How can I understand,
While my finger turns a bookleaf,
That for him seeds and quick sips
Of water are enough?

Narwhal Tusk

The narwhal, forcing
His way through water,
Turns his tusk,
Furrowing its ivory*
By his own vigour.

Equally our worries
Pierce the future,
Spiralling ahead
To form a torque
Just from the stress
Of years through which we move.

We go and we are gone.

While the sea folds inward,
Leaving no mark:
Like air in a bird's wake.

Eumenides

The Furies danced from happiness,
    Hand in hand,
    Knowing they controlled great
    Houses, broke them, hounded men:
    Each step, each twirl of hem so light
    In its revenge and hate.

Today we know that fateful band
    Is most determined,
    Most intent
    To castigate
    And give, not just one family,
    But each poor soul, distress.

Gone is Athena* the great goddess,
    She who forced them to relent.

Rapunzel

    May I be
    Reminded of Rapunzel;

Her blue rampion;
Her prince blinded by thorns
And how her tears
Made him fair and whole—
Each time I wander,
Stupid with fears,
Over the night's
Desert of despair.

No Rusty Cry

No rusty cry
From corncrakes in a field of wheat—
Their thin legs could outrun
And would defy
The reaper's clack
That spoke for summer's
Lazy heat.
Combine harvesters
Have come along
And must be best.

Though scavenging the past is wrong—
I can't go back,
I have no rest—
Where is the future's drowsy sun?
What will be fresh, untainted, blest?

In Praise of Fashion

A waist small
    As a bull-leaper's
    Or a prince of Crete;
    His belt studded
    Like that of Orion.

Elegance in death, in constellation.
Who can fault
What will enlarge
The night, then vault,
It seems, tall as noon heat?

Were There a Choice

Were there a choice:
The smoothest painted Claude or say
Guercino glade and forest, quiet
As glass, with no twig stirring, not a pulse
Of air, as in a coma
When one scarcely breathes
But feels a calm beyond all telling;
Creatures without help and hounded
As we are, I know—having all but made
That journey to its end—
Find it by far the easiest way to go.

And yet you might prefer
A small, bitter flurry of wind
Battling the tide, its touch pocking
Harbour water into cross-currents and then
Slapping the sea-wall
As you set out, with a stubbed
Dip of dinghy oars—excited
By a smell of kelp, tar,
Wet ropes, half-rusted iron—to the moored
Sailboat waiting for you
With its coffin-like and solid planking.

Nearing the End

As the door
Closes, so
A narrow
Slice of light
Diminishes
On the floor.

Age knows haste,
Knows fright.
It wants to flee
From Nahum's words:
She is empty,
And void, and waste.

Baby Song

O cradled daughter:
No Dancing-water*
Will make you young
When your dimpled arm
And rounded neck
Look scrawny and wrung.

Provided no harm,
My darling queen,
Should come in between;
No hint of such wreck
As I've suffered and seen.
Now I'll hush my tongue.

The Oath

Hand to hand, foot to foot,
Knee to knee, breast to breast
In darkness: a masonic rite.
Would that all lovers
Kept their oath so well.

COCKATRICE
AND BASILISK

1983

Cockatrice and Basilisk

Cockatrice and Basilisk
Lithe and brisk
Find me nightly.

How they sting
And how they stare!
Each unsightly

Thing I've done
In the past, everywhere,
Is no longer glazed by sun;

Their Monster-play
Will taunt, then flay
My soul until it's wholly bare.

We Were Bright Beings

We were bright beings
Made of wave and plunging light.
In a surprise of seas we sauntered
Who now dry our scaly nets
Over the rocks.

The hot reminders
Of what's gone, the cold revulsion
From what's done:
O lucky wave. O lucky leaf
Where autumn woods must smoulder

Till put out by rain
And pigeons clip the empty air.

Caterpillar

In the sweet arbour of your twig
Can you work out, you caterpillar,
Some wide allegory
Or unique philosophy
To fit that bole
You climbed, all hump-back, up the tree?

From tides of intellect,
Or else the White Clown's vanity
Which thinks a soul should glitter,
We—who cannot tell how many
Galaxies are neighbour
To another; what is minimal or big;
What's crooked, straight;
(Just as you, caterpillar-insect,
Cannot count what leaves you ate)—

Still brandish high-flown thoughts. We,
In pride and brain, still lack your
Miracle of power
To become evasive,
Beautiful fragility
For one short summer's fate.

Rose and Creed*

If *Rosa Mundi*, a *gallica*, varied
In double pinkness, should be confused
(As often happens) with the fine

York and Lancaster, blushing two colours, a *damascene*,
    Each of them uttering glory:
Why should this change in detail maim our wholeness,
    Slashed and striped
        As it is
        By discord
    Of human disunity?

    Think how fists crashed on a table
    While curses were hurled, one at another
    In turn, by bishops in their
Nicaean committee, called for hammering out
    A Creed to annihilate—
But for all time—that hateful Arian heresy.
      And the result?
        Stupendous,
        Most loving,
    Ineffable poetry.

Keeping House Together

1

    So let Augustine
Be uncaring: look at
    Jerome weeping
At the fall of Rome.

2

    In spring, tender
Vine-leaves hook in a trellis,
    Filtering sun
Over a peasant skull

3

    Whose friend, alongside,
Tries to gull; enrage;
    Attack, from Guilt;
Fetch blood. A flask's pushed back.

4

Quarrels begun
Like this will often heal
Because each threat
Carries a partial Bliss.

5

But Pride? Oh, she'll
Delight that feathers which warmed
Leda, touched her
In sleep, Zeus playing stud:

6

While Age, both jilt
And pandar, asks that Right
And Wrong keep house
Together, feel at home.

Hazards

Among the hazards that infect the world,
Tough Aeschylus, who'd fought
In Persian wars,
Died when an eagle—as we know—
Thought his head, shining-bald,
A stone. And dropped
That tortoise on it from a height.

Bitter for Sophocles
At ninety, when his son
Hauled him to court
To prove him both incapable and imbecile.
Father recited from his new,
Unplayed *Oedipus at Colónus*.
Suit dismissed.

Or take Euripides, guest
Of that cultivated man,

King Archelaus of Macedonia—
Ripped into pieces by a pack
Of hunting-dogs.
Eagle, son, or savage hounds:
Which was the worst? I know.

Blaze and Blackness

Feu feu
Fire in the universe.

Foraminifera, diatoms, plankton—
Far the most numerous of creatures—
At a touch
Will light black seas.

Pascal was face to face with the Unknown
For two whole hours: the summit of his life.
Fire, fire. God is the God of Abraham, Isaac and Jacob,
Not of the philosophers. And may I never be cut off
From Jesus Christ. Peace, joy and certitude.
This he remembered, wrote, and hid in a sewn
Pouch they found in his doublet-lining after death.

Might this foretell
The finish of our globe?
Or how men cheat,
As did those Patriarchs?

But then, our own
Dame Julian of Norwich,
Visionary, too, said:
All wil be wel and all manner of thing wil be wel.

Sheer light.
Such dark.

Dachau, Gulag, hundreds of crucifixions stretched
By Romans along Palestinian roads; that heartbreak
In the Aramaic
Mother-tongue:
Eloi, Eloi, lama sabacthani.

We may be held by the barbed wire of cruelty,
Or walls of logic,
Or a hedge
Enclosing gardens of sweet love.
Should wire-cutters or mason's pick
Or clippers
Get to work and open
These a fraction,
Would it be right to think
Life is a faulty ledge
Of overall and pure irrationality?

A Frightened Creature

I

Clearly, I take delight
In any smattering
About poor, cold
Antigone;
Zeus as an infant, bawling
In his Cretan cave;
Teiresias; or crossroads ruled by Hecate
At midnight.
But, when these come into my home
Or I near theirs,
I know considerable fear.
Legends brimming with wonder
Pain us like a wound—more so than some big
Chronicle of actuality.

Out of a tome
Giving the stories, names leap free.
Characters, in force, have faces shining
From their grief; from exultation; fright
Or lack
Of it: such as Hippolytus, young prig,
Who dares
To manage without love.
Here I step back—
I made a blunder:
Blind Teiresias the seer,
This womaned-man, has cheeks so grave
And furrowed, they reflect
No light.

3

Each year
I'm more afraid. Is this the due seed of Age,
And Age's right?

Ferryman

Charon beckons, while his other hand
Grasps the white and fraying oar
He sculls with from the stern,

And hears crowds shuffle; till the piteous band
Flinches when it feels his shore:
Appalled at no return.

Loving

Do you prefer your loving
Warm and huddled
As a fold of sheep?

Or better, a lost language:
Hope and excitement
In its deciphering?

'It is not such heinous matter
To fall afflicted,
As being to lie dejected,'

Wrote St. Chrysostom.
Is this, perhaps,
Your heart's true state?

Destination

The ladder has been left slanted
In a half-clipped hornbeam
And a rake's teeth
Will no more scratch gently across the gravel.

Rows of defective houses
Wait until they're crushed
In rubble-dust.
To slums, or unkempt gardens, all of us travel.

Homage

I
Roots of *acaulis*, bluest
Of all gentians, have
So small a place to go
Where they can stretch: this in no way impedes
Their trumpeting, their brilliant and benumbing glow.

Camargue, whose grit and sand
Reach the world's rim: oh,
Welcome, speckled snipe,
Watching me quite still and closely from
A tussock, with no fear, your black and round eye liquid.

3

Dusk in a garden mutes
All colours, till we know
How purity, extreme
And blinding, like a virtue unexcelled,
Can blow from that old rose *Blanc Double de Coubert.*

4

Through a thin mist, one hears
The clash of a great castle's
Throw and overthrow;
Then sees a different and Georgian grace.
Homage to Powerscourt, now merely walls and ash.

Easy Felled

Kindness, even more than fleshly
Love, has compelled
And ever undone me;

Lies and all wickedness that I know
Must blot the sun,
Will torture me;

Gregorian chant: its ebb and flow
Makes the heart falter,
Rise again;

But by words, by written words, I'm easy
Felled as a dove
On an African tree.

Thou Shalt Not Carry a Fox's Tooth

1

Thou shalt not carry a fox's tooth
As do the Amorites.
A dried frog-bone
Or striped pebble
Will serve as well.
Boys with talismans in a pocket
Know every charm;
They are augurs, too,
Interpreting what signs tell
Of good luck.

2

For them, the future
Lies in the present. Here
All is clarity
As in this small, quick-moving
Stream, whose past
Begins again, smelling of mint;
While a water-wagtail alights
On a flat stone
Between the ripples.

3

If such entirety,
Such lack of harm
Should be the truth,
Also a hint
Of grace, then grace
Is almost too much happiness to bear.

Urgent

Villages pass under the plough
In England, where there was plague,
And lets time slide over parishes

The way hedges are torn out.
Bulldozers flatten a hill:
Even continents slip.
Everything must elide or kill
As the wild aurochs died;
And our elms. We have
Barely a minute now.

Uncut Hedges

Young, needing the smell of peace,
    I turned to ditches
Where high eglantine and dog-rose
    Used their lease
In modesty; their stems caught
    By every flower
And weed that fought with equal valour,
    Mixed and knit
Disorderly. I was not taught,
    Was without wit,
To guess what Herculean labour
    Went to quell
Competitors and so promote
    Both life and power;
What counter-plot was fortunate;
    Which microbe, mould
And insect, weevil, worm or stoat
    Let a thin root
Find space to show its common bloom
    In royal state.

    Now that I'm old,
        I see
Life's tangled jealousy
    Alas too well,
    Alas too late.

Song of a Past Scullery-Maid

Let origano—so
The mistress calls wild marjoram—be
Stuck a-plenty
In my window.

Worn out by soap and scrub-brush,
And my naked feet
Bruised by stone flags,
I want the smell of the old gardener's sweet
Potting-shed: there hide my rags
And arms in its dim, earthy hush.

And when at last I go
And need some blooms to smother me,
If season's right, may parson see
They're from the wild white gean tree.*

Boxwood

Faint and also pungent;
Honeyed but with a tang:
Clipped boxwood in the sun exhales
Its quite intoxicating breath.

What can be likened to this
Contradiction, to such
Humble potency? If we were
Told, 'Go look in your own selves'—

Not only mine, but boundless
Characters, would then
Be found along that honed blade-edge
Of strength, and timorous withdrawal.

174

All but Gone from Bermuda

Those little ground-doves
Pecking along pathways,
Waddling in dust.

Perched on the lowest twig,
A chick-of-the-village
With his yellow eye so big
And most enquiring.

Herald of June:
That high-pitched twittering
From tropic-birds—the longtail—
Now too few.

O my lost loves.

If you must
Go, as always
Happens, or have gone so soon,
Nothing can twist or harm
My power of recalling
A big charm
Of goldfinches, deftly fluttering
Around pale
Thistledown, in a wild spot I knew.

Child

To know time from a closing pimpernel;
Sniff mushrooms at day-break
Where donkeys graze;
Chew sorrel for its salt; eat mallow-pods
Tasting of cheese;

Feel for a hen's well-hidden egg
That warms a cupped hand;
Get torn while learning
How imperially
Great ripened brambles glitter . . .
Yes, indeed, poor Croesus.

Unending Search

When we were humours—
Sanguine or phlegmatic,
Filled with black bile, or else choleric—
Where was the personal and ordinary,
Quite familiar self that changes colour daily?

Or when fit for hell,
Why was each rescuing angel
So far off? Most orderly
Arranged in rank, each had as well as halo,
Delicate bare feet, above the Trinity.

Now that we learn
How little we can know,
It might be better to return:
Illuminated Books of Hours, or fresco
Could be our help; in medicine, chiefly herbs and rumours.

No Instructions

To give quite freely or else hold,
To be amazed, or bold:

How can we judge? Connect
Our body's bias, dogma, sect?

Once, Dr Dee's* high-polished coal
Played mirror. We have quasar or black hole

For marvel. Not a thing
Is understood. And, ripening,

We die the moment that we start to learn
Just what we are, just where to turn.

Notes

page

4   the Euxine From Argonaut legend, probably based on the discovery by some early Greek expedition which found that the people of Colchis panned for gold by catching lake water in sheep-fleeces.

5   golden bird *L'oiseau de feu* of legend, perhaps due to knowledge of golden pheasants in the Persian hills or thereabouts.

5   bright-cottoned ebonies Up to 1939 nearly all West African women from Dakar to the River Niger wore multi-colored Manchester-made cotton robes and head knots. The manner of their stylishly tied head-gear distinguished each tribe. Nigerians dyed their cottons with home-grown indigo alone.

8   compass legs Dividers used in calculating longitude.

9   St. Jerome The supposed illegality of teaching Hebrew forced St. Jerome to hide the fact that he was being taught it for his translation of the Vulgate.

15   Mimas A member of the Rodd family, posted in Athens, sailed a small boat along Odysseus's presumed route. He was delighted to find that the offshore wind blew from Mimas, just as described by Homer.

16   Dargle The infant source of a tributary to the Liffey begins with the highest waterfall in the United Kingdom and Ireland, and is in the Powerscourt demesne.

19   *Beat Drum, Beat Heart*   It so happens that the long poem
      Beat Drum, Beat Heart was written many years be-
      fore World War II, and had only six lines added
      during that war to bring it more up to date.

21   *li*   Chinese unit of distance.

22   youths To whom a lute, a rose   The sea-battle of
      Lepanto in 1571, when the Turks were stopped from
      over-running all Europe: the fashion for young men
      on the European side was to wear guelder-roses as
      ornaments on their shoes.

22   Long March   Mao's Long March began in October 1934
      in Kiangsi with 100,000 men, ending 368 days later in
      Shensi (west of Peking) with 50,000 men, having
      covered 6000 miles.

25   a lad   *Tobias and the Angel*, Botticelli.

26   With some of the brambles ripe   The battle of Vinegar
      Hill, eighteenth century, during Ireland's prolonged
      War of Independence.

27   Minories   Aldgate and Minories in the City of London.
      A soldier in Allenby's campaign speaking.

28   one who led us   Author had T. E. Lawrence in mind as
      leader.

28   'I a Venetian . . .'   Battle in which Genoa defeated
      Venice.

29   Brian, the old king   Brian Boru, King of Munster, killed
      in the eleventh century. At this time the Irish were
      fighting the Danes, who had occupied Dublin.

29   Sir John Chandos   Admirably courageous knight, who
      saved the life of the Black Prince.

30   *Hector, Judith* and *Lahire*   Some of the court cards in
      continental packs.

32   Scamander   River near Hissarlik, site of historic Troy.

36   a morning walked alone   The whole passage is an ac-

curate description of the seventh Lord Powerscourt's making of the Italianate terraced part of Powerscourt garden.

38   the twin Horses These life-sized Pegasi, heraldic supporters of the family's coat-of-arms, guard the pleasure-garden's ornamental lake.

39   Amen Corner The dome of St. Paul's Cathedral housed a library, in a room carved by Grinling Gibbons, where for a few pence one could see one of the finest collections of lay books, including this first edition of Chaucer, detailed account books of the rebuilding of St. Paul's, subscription lists after the Great Fire, and many treasures of great interest to bibliophiles. Next door, in the Muniment Room, are documents and Royal seals of early English Kings, many of whom were crowned in old St. Paul's before the Norman Conquest.

The Cathedral used to be the centre of social life for the community, and Londoners referred to it as our Paul's. Wren designed the steps leading up to the present building to prevent the entry of donkeys loaded with merchandise; but wishing to perpetuate the best of the old tradition, he originally planned his Cathedral with small rooms instead of side-chapels, where City Guilds could meet. This was turned down.

39   the lens grinder Baruch Spinoza, the philosopher praised beyond all others by Bertrand Russell, died from tuberculosis due to his secondary occupation of lens grinding.

42   By saint The island of Ensay in the Outer Hebrides is roughly two miles long and half a mile across but has a very small ruin which is known as St. Columba's Cathedral.

42   Glendalough Seven ruined early Christian churches in a monastic settlement in County Wicklow. The hermit St. Kevin lived in a hollowed space in the vertical rock above the lake.

43   Armageddon   Fortifications dug up at Megiddo revealed
          the Biblical 'Armageddon.'

50   Erzulie   Voodoo goddess of love in Haitian rites.

51   Aquinas   Having finished his monumental *Summa Theo-
          logica*, Aquinas had a mystical experience. He then
          said, "All I have written is as straw," and refused
          to pronounce again on religious matters.

53   '*Pourrvou que cela dourre* . . .' Favorite remark of
          Buonaparte's mother when neighbors informed her
          of her son's victories.

54   Persian Arrows   Excavations at Thermopylae show the
          truth of Herodotus' statement that the Persian host
          was so vast that its arrows obscured the sun. The
          wall of Phocias was found and repairs in it mentioned
          by Herodotus, also the stone posts of the gates from
          which the name Thermopylae was derived. No
          arrowheads here (from where the Spartans charged
          the Persians, and Leonidas was killed) but a huge
          mass of them was found in the hill to which his
          three hundred withdrew.

54   the Angel   A country legend in a certain part of France
          of Eve and the Garden of Eden.

55   She ran from the vast house   Lady Ottoline Morrell, half
          sister of the then Duke of Portland, ran away from
          Welbeck Abbey to Edinburgh University, having
          first made herself a cloak lined with a mass of pockets
          into which she put the best part of a small library.

56   A third one   A latter-day Miss Havisham, whom I knew
          well in a sub-tropical island. When young, she fell
          in love with a young actor, and he with her. Her
          Victorian father intercepted all letters between them.
          When they met again, many years after, he was mar-
          ried. Neither of them ever got over the shock, and
          when telling me the full story in her eighties she
          still trembled from emotion.

57   Kind Dorothy Dorothy Wordsworth, who had an un-requited love for Coleridge.

57   Mary's letters, sweet Wordsworth's wife, married late in life; her most affectionate letters to him having been only recently discovered.

58   Such small figurines Terracotta figures, from a tomb in Myrina, of turbaned and dancing winged Erotes, seen by me in the Boston Museum of Fine Arts.

62   Magdala In Biblical times, a small village on the Sea of Galilee. Home of Mary Magdalene.

77   Libyan Arabs The Senussi.

78   Clonmacnois A Monastic university founded in the sixth century by St. Ciaran, a centre of scholarship and manuscript making, repeatedly raided by Danes, then Irishmen, and finally sacked by the English.

79   *Ross Abbey* The scene of great happiness in the author's childhood.

80   *Four Men's Desire* Biblical scholarship now recognises the likelihood of four Johns:

        (1) John the Baptist

        (2) John the Apostle (son of Zebedee and brother of James), who was probably martyred with his brother in A.D. 44

        (3) John the Evangelist (John of Ephesus), who may have lived at the end of the first century and is thought to have belonged to a Sadducean, high priestly family. The last chapter of the Gospel is generally agreed to be an editorial addition. Internal evidence shows the impossibility of the Fourth Gospel's author being John the Apostle living to a ripe old age at Ephesus. It is believed to be the work of '*Un juif hellénisant, inspiré de Philon d'Alex-andrie, qui connait les Synoptiques, mais n'en fait point cas. C'est un théologien mystique, non un his-torien.*'—S. Reinach. '*Les récits de Jean ne sont pas*

de l'histoire mais une contemplation de l'Evangile; ses discours sont des méditations théologiques sur le mystère du salut.'—Prof. Loisy

(4) St. John the Divine (John of Patmos). The Book of Revelation was probably written towards the end of the first century. 'He expressed his thoughts and feelings in barbarous Greek, disfigured by Semitic use. His style is conclusive against his having been the John who wrote the Fourth Gospel.'—Dr. Barnes, late Bishop of Birmingham.

81 Jason It is possible that the tale of Jason and the wild bulls originated in his taming an aurochs for farm work, the European aurochs being a variety of American buffalo which once roamed Eastern Europe. It is now extinct except for a carefully preserved small herd.

81 cahòw Bird indigenous to Bermuda (whose population was founded from survivors of Sir George Somers' shipwreck in 1609, who found Bermuda teeming with wildlife). Cahòws made an unnatural sounding shriek (giving the island a reputation for being filled with strange sounds and supernatural beings— *The Tempest*) and were so tame that sailors caught them by hand and found them delicious eating. They were thought to have become extinct, until a breeding pair or two were recently discovered on a tiny uninhabited rock. The birds are now carefully protected.

81 gnomon Geometrically, a figure which can be added to so that the resultant whole still retains the original shape. To make a gnomonic rectangle, take a figure whose sides are in the proportion of 1 to .618; add a square to the longer side; the whole new rectangle will have the same shape as the first. Add a square to the longer side of the new figure, and so on. The spiral which can be traced from the boundaries of such figures is the spiral of the whelk and nautilus, turban shell and snail. Not only do most shells grow in this gnomonic fashion, but the most common ar-

rangements of leaves round a stem, sun-flower petals, or scales in a fir-cone, follow the ratio of:

0:1, 1:2, 3:5, 8:13, 21:34, 55:89, 144: etc.

(See Sir D'Arcy Thompson's *On Growth and Form*). This is the series of what are sometimes called the Fibonacci numbers, which can be written as:

$$\frac{0}{1}, \frac{1}{2}, \frac{3}{5}, \frac{8}{13}, \frac{21}{34}, \text{ etc.}$$

If these fractions are worked out, they are seen to get nearer and nearer to 0.618, in other words, to converge to the number mentioned earlier. This number (0.618) was well known to the ancients, who called it the *sectio divina* or Golden Mean.

The mechanical stresses of growth call for a special solution, if the organism that grows is to keep its orderly and original shape; and it is curious and lovely to see with what frequency and elegance Nature provides the gnomon as the answer to anarchy.

82 pedlar, diplomat, landlord, peasant Trying to discover what origins I might have had on both sides of the family who were roughly contemporary in the six-teenth or seventeenth centuries, I came up with the following: (a) 'landlord': a Cornishman, Stephen Braddon of Treworgey St. Gennys, M.P. for Bossiney 1558 to 1565; (b) 'peasant': an Irish cattle-raider successful enough to build himself a small and now demolished castle called Bally Ard in County Offaly in the centre of Ireland; (c) 'diplomat': a Financial Governor and Adviser to Ferdinand and Isabel of Spain, and their lifelong friend; (d) 'pedlar': a Jewish pedlar in the Alsatian town of Colmar (then French).

83 stanzas 5 and 7 of "Origins" The following suggestions are taken from Sir Reginald Fessenden's *The Deluged Civilization of the Caucasian Isthmus*, whose specula-tions on the Northern Caucasian origin of man as

the original metallurgist have had the support—though for different reasons—of Breasted and Flinders Petrie.

The Caspian, Balkasch and Aral Seas are the remains, now dried up, of a far larger sea which was once connected with the Arctic Ocean and also, via the Manytsch lakes, with the Sea of Azov and the Black Sea. When this larger sea was in being, the earliest metal-working civilization was possibly established in the Northern Caucasus. Mankind would have had no incentive to leave this locality, bounded northward by ice, to the west by a vast morass infested by mosquitoes (Herodotus' 'bees'), to the east by the Everburning Fields (Baku oilfields) and the sea, and to the south by the seemingly impassable range of the Caucasus; also rich in fire (spontaneously ignitable naphtha), metal ores, timber, alluvial soil, irrigating streams, useful animals, fruit, and grain. The mountain of Iron and Brass nearby was Mt. Thammizeria or Tamischieria.

With the melting of the ice-cap, the enlarged Caspian (mentioned above) flooded westward and forced the discovery of the Pass of Dariel (or Erebus) near Mt. Kasbek, through the Caucasus and into a region known in Semitic times as Aidon or, more exactly, East Aidon. Erebus, a five hundred feet deep cleft, runs due north and south, so that its forbidding defile is dark even in summer. Its fortified gates (Iron Gates) are said to have been placed there by King Aidoneus (king of Aidon). Beyond the pass, the western and middle portion of the valley was called *Aidon* by the Semites, Aethiopia by the Phoenicians, and later, Colchis by the Greeks. The middle portion, East Aidon—walled in by mountains on all four sides and into which the gate opened—is the *Paradeisos,* or enclosed park, of the Septuagint, and the Garden of Eden of the Semites. The eastern third of the valley, through which the River Alizon flows, is called *Elysion* by the Greeks. The vegetation of the *Garden of Aidon* was luxuriant and dense, with fruit-trees bearing wild fruit, all-year-round flowers and thick pasturage. Genesis and Strabo (whose great-uncle was Governor of Colchis) both state that very heavy dew watered portions where little rain fell, so there was never any drought.

Tree of Life: The Golden Apples of the Hesperides: Greek tradition says the fruit was coloured gold and like an apple, prolonged life but was guarded by a dragon. Ezekiel says the tree was guarded by cherubim (Kirubi) with four feet and four wings, like dragons. Creatures which would answer this description are now found in Malaya, in the form of flying lizards: Amagidae, or *draco volans*. They are brightly coloured, look like a snake when their wings are folded, and are partial to *Citrus medica*. 'Upon thy belly thou shalt go' has meaning when applied to these beautiful flying reptiles.

Citrus Medica has remarkable healing properties for wounds; it helps the intestinal tract and has a high vitamin content.

Tree of Knowledge of Good and Evil: this is a variety of *Datura*. It acts like a drug to induce great mental acuity, followed by depression; it is highly appetising, an aphrodisiac, and can also give violent delirium. Fumes of it when burnt have the same effect.

'He placed at the east of the Garden of Eden the Kirubi, and the flame of a sword which turneth every way.' The sword was probably a fired oilwell in what is now the Baku district, visible for great distances as it wavered from side to side.

Wailing for Thammuz, which later degenerated into the lowest of orgies, was originally a reenactment of Queen Ashirta of the Chalybes bewailing the drowning in the deluge of Thammuz her husband, and his armies. (Other floods are historically known.)

91   *A Kite's Dinner* The title of this collection is taken from Quarles's emblems. It is attributed to Hugo, *Liber de Anima*. The following is an extract from a

letter from Fr. A. Gwynn, S.J., of Dublin: 'I have found the very words which Quarles quotes in a treatise *De Interiori Domo*, printed in Migne as a work wrongly attributed to St. Bernard (P.L. 184, col. 543). This treatise is sometimes given as part of Liber de Anima, attributed to Hugh of St. Victor. It was probably written by a Cistercian monk of the twelfth century. Here are the words (loc. sit.): "De Interiori Domo, cap. 72: O custos cordis, quam modicum et cupidum cor habes! Parvum est et magna cupit. Vix ad unius milvi refectionem sufficere posset, et totus mundus ei non sufficit."

97   ceremony old as dreams   The anniversary of the return of St. Mark's bones from Alexandria, celebrated each 500 years. This is by Venetian reckoning.

105   Burial ground   Written before Powerscourt, which had an adjacent burial ground for the family, was accidentally destroyed by fire in 1974.

107   among roses and quails   The Misses Eden, travelling through India in the mid-nineteenth century, called it a country of roses and quails; they also referred to this local legend.

107   Abu Zulaymah   Sir Richard Burton, *Pilgrimage to Al Medinah and Meccah.*

107   Juz Asaf of Kashmir   A tradition, still vivid in Burton's day, of a first-century cave-dwelling, solitary saint in India, called Juz Asaf, who, he imagines, might conceivably be Christ, nursed back to health by Joseph of Arimathea and in a mood of deception travelling north; to become revered in India. This seemingly outlandish theory has had the support of many high-powered ecclesiastical and historical savants.

113   asphodel   Most travellers seem disappointed by this flower. They appear not to expect a subdued, rather ghostly, greyish pink.

115   *Tinker*   Present-day dwindling bands of true tinkers, believed to be descendants of people of the Indus

Valley who stayed in the Byzantine Empire as metal workers, during their slow westward migration.

116   "Judge not . . ." Quotations are fragments from Rabbi Hillel, c. 75 B.C.–A.D. 10.

125   geas Particular prohibition put on heroes in Irish folklore. Pronounced "gaysh."

126   bézoar According to the 1678 edition of *Tavernier's Journals* (Bk. II, Ch. 2) bézoar was a gum secreted by a special breed of Indian she-goat. This substance was thought excessively valuable.

128   A screech-owl Lilith, the name of Adam's supposed first wife, is the Hebrew word for screech-owl.

129   when a conch shell brays As was once the custom when Bermudian fishermen came ashore with their catch.

133   See note on Clonmacnois on page 183.

142   They fly back to their hives Swarming bees are affected by an audio-frequency of 960 cycles a second (which occurs when metal objects are banged together); this sound impels bees to stop whatever they are doing and start feeding each other with honey; swarming bees rush back to their hive for this purpose.

142   Miltonic See *Paradise Lost*, beginning of Bk. III.

151   That black pebble *Ogam*, Tome XIV, July–September 1962, *Oracular and Speaking Stones in Celtic Britain* by Ellen Ettlinger. This article quotes from a letter from T. H. Mason of Dublin, dated 13 February 1950: 'A black stone, lying close to the sea . . . received worship in the Hebrides till a comparatively recent date. Sir Walter Scott says it was supposed to be oracular, and to answer whatever questions might be asked. . . . The people never approached it without certain formalities.'

155   Furrowing its ivory See Sir D'Arcy Thompson's *Growth and Form*.

156   Athena See *Oresteia*, Aeschylus.

159   Dancing-water   A fairy elixir to give back lost youth.

164   *Rose and Creed*   The Nicene Creed (used in the Communion Service) was mainly formulated after bitter arguments at the Council held at Nicea, A.D. 325.

174   gean tree   A common name for the European wild cherry.

177   Dr. Dee   Queen Elizabeth's famous seer as well as a noted philosopher-scientist-mathematician-physician.